THE

REFERENCE

SHELF

REPRESENTATIVE

AMERICAN SPEECHES,

1992–1993

edited by OWEN PETERSON
Professor, Department of Speech Communication
Louisiana State University

THE REFERENCE SHELF

Volume 65 Number 6

THE H. W. WILSON COMPANY

New York   1993

THE REFERENCE SHELF

The books in this series contain reprints of articles, excerpts from books, and addresses on current issues and social trends in the United States and other countries. There are six separately bound numbers in each volume, all of which are generally published in the same calendar year. One number is a collection of recent speeches; each of the others is devoted to a single subject and gives background information and discussion from various points of view, concluding with a comprehensive bibliography that contains books and pamphlets and abstracts of additional articles on the subject. Books in the series may be purchased individually or on subscription.

The Library of Congress has cataloged this serial title as follows:

Representative American speeches. 1937/38–
    New York, H. W. Wilson Co.
      v. 21 cm.—(The Reference shelf)
    Annual.
    Indexes:
      Author index: 1937/38–1959/60, with 1959/60;
      1960/61–1969/70, with 1969/70; 1970/71–1979/80,
      with 1979/80; 1980/81–1989/90, with 1990.
    Editors: 1937/38–1958/59, A. C. Baird.—1959/60–1969/70, L.
    Thonssen.—1970/71–1979/80, W. W. Braden.—1980/81– O.
    Peterson.
    ISSN 0197-6923 Representative American speeches.
      1. Speeches, addresses, etc., American. 2. Speeches, addresses, etc.
    I. Baird, Albert Craig, 1883–1979 ed. II. Thonssen,
    Lester, 1904– ed. III. Braden, Waldo Warder, 1911–1991 ed.
    IV. Peterson, Owen, 1924– ed. V. Series.
    PS668.B3   815.5082   38-27962
                                            MARC-S

    Library of Congress [8503r85]rev4

Printed in the United States of America

CONTENTS

SHAPING THE FUTURE

LEST WE FORGET

PREFACE

During most of 1992–1993, public speaking in the United States focused on the presidential and congressional elections. While speakers addressed a variety of topics—some old and a few new—election issues dominated public discussion.

Highlighting the early part of 1992 were the contest for the Democratic party's presidential nomination and the challenge to President George Bush by the conservative wing of the Republican Party. Enlivening the political scene was the on-and-off candidacy of independent challenger, multimillionaire H. Ross Perot.

The parties' national conventions, carefully choreographed by political veterans and professional consultants, produced little oratory of note, although some Democratic observers felt that the stridency of the attacks by speakers at the Republican convention may have harmed their cause. After much haggling, the two parties, and the Perot campaign, agreed to hold three nationally televised debates, two involving the three presidential candidates and one with the vice-presidential contenders. There were two notable differences from prior presidential campaigns: Mr. Perot's huge personal expenditure, largely for large blocks of television prime time; and the extensive talk-show appearances by all of the contenders.

When the election was over statistics showed an increase in voter turnout from 51% in 1988, to 55% in 1992, the highest since 1972. (This percentage, however, is still far below that of most other western democracies, in which voter turnout usually ranges between 65% and 80%). Whether the increase in voter turnout could be attributed to better communication or simply public frustration with government is unclear.

The discouraging but not surprising news is that campaigning for Congress has become more expensive than ever. Candidates for the both houses of Congress spent a total of $678 million on their election campaigns—53% more than was spent in the 1990 Congressional races.

The dominant political issue of 1992–1993 was, of course, the economy, including the related concerns over the cost and availability of medical care and the size of cuts in military spending. Among other issues in public debate were the ban on homosexuals serving in the military, crime, violence, drug abuse, AIDS, education, racism and abortion. 1992 also saw a focus of address on several issues related to freedom of speech, including: "hate" speech, political correctness, and academic freedom.

In preparing this collection of speeches, I am deeply indebted to many people for their help. I am especially appreciative of the research contributions of Lyman Hunt, who provided valuable information about the speakers, speeches, audiences and occasions. Once again, Kacie Wolfe helped obtain speeches as well as type the manuscripts and introductions. I thank Ginger Conrad and Lisa Landry for their continued cooperation and help. My Louisiana State University colleagues; Stephen Cooper, Gresdna Doty, Mary Frances Hopkins, Harold Mixon and James Traynham again provided helpful insights and suggestions. I also wish to acknowledge the support of my department chairman Dr. Andrew King.

Others who helped in various ways in preparation of this collection are Thomas Bauer, Samuel L. Becker, Liz Burns, Theodore R. Couch, Jodi J. Csar, Kimberly R. Dillinger, Holly Folk, Senator James M. Jeffords, Robert C. Jeffrey, Jeanann M. Pock, Rosalie Seemaun, Senator Paul Simon, Kristin Simone, Laurel Stavis, John Trohoske and Harris Wofford.

OWEN PETERSON

Baton Rouge, Louisiana
June 4, 1993

INAUGURAL ADDRESS[1]
WILLIAM J. CLINTON[2]

Of what importance is the inauguration of a new president? According to Representative Lee Hamilton:

The inauguration of a new President is one of the great rituals of American democracy—trumpets, poetry, choirs, military bands, prayers, stirring oratory, and, most impressive, a vast sea of onlookers—all brought into the living rooms of millions of Americans by television. . . . The importance of the inauguration lies in what it symbolizes after a contentious and messy political campaign: the unquestioned acceptance by the winner and the loser and of all the American people of the continuity of the American government. A President's inaugural address is important because it sets the tone of his administration. (*Congressional Record*, January 27, 1993, p. E196)

On January 20, 1993, William Jefferson Clinton became the forty-second President of the United States. His swearing in, the ceremony and festivities accompanying it, and his address faithfully reflected and fulfilled the symbolic requirements of a presidential inauguration as they are described by Mr. Hamilton.

The five days of frenetic inaugural activities began on January 17 and included festivals, concerts, parades, and ten balls with tickets at $125. The total cost of the events—$25 million—was actually less than most recent inaugurals and was paid for entirely by private contributions and through the sale of tickets and souvenirs.

Inaugural day itself, January 20, began with the Clinton family attending a prayer service at the Metropolitan A.M.E. Church at 8 A.M. This was followed by a White House reception for the Clintons given by outgoing President Bush and his wife. The inaugural ceremony took place on a crisp winter day at 11:30 A.M. on the west front of the Capitol before a crowd of 300,000. It began with an invocation by the Reverend Billy Graham, fol-

---

[1]Delivered from the western facade of the Capitol, Washington, D.C. at noon on January 20, 1993.

[2]For biographical note, see Appendix.

lowed by the administering of the oath of office to Vice-President
Albert Gore by retired Supreme Court Justice Thurgood Marshall. Thomas L. Friedman of the *New York Times* describes the
remainder of ceremony as follows:

> The 46-year-old Governor of Arkansas, 18 months ago a virtual un-
> known to most Americans and a longshot for the White House, took the
> oath of office under a clear blue sky from Chief Justice William H. Rehn-
> quist. President George Herbert Walker Bush, who had once seemed sure
> to win a second term, watched stoically from his seat on the Capitol steps.
> Under Mr. Clinton's left hand, his wife, Hillary, held a King James
> Bible given to Mr. Clinton by his grandmother. His 12-year-old daughter,
> Chelsea, stood at his right as he uttered the traditional oath at 11:58 A.M.
> Eastern time. He then spoke for 14 minutes to a sea of people, flowing
> down from the flat-draped Western facade of the Capitol to the Washing-
> ton monument. . . .
> In a speech with the recurring theme of renewal, Mr. Clinton im-
> plored at one point: "To renew America we must be bold. We must do
> what no generation has had to do before. . . .
> Mr. Clinton's Inaugural Address, far more compact than the lengthy
> oratory of his long 1988 Democratic National Convention speech, was
> informal and almost conversational. (January 21, 1993, p. 1).

It is of interest that President Clinton, who has a penchant for
verbosity and a history of diminishing the effectiveness of crucial
speeches by his long-windedness, chose to write his inaugural
speech himself, refusing the help of speechwriters. Aides reported that he spent considerable time reviewing inaugural speeches
of past presidents, paying special attention to Abraham Lincoln's
second inaugural address, and had rehearsed the draft in front of
a Teleprompter. (Gwen Ifill, *New York Times*, January 19, 1993,
p. A7).

Response to the Inaugural Address was generally favorable.
In an editorial, the *Chicago Tribune* observed:

> President Bill Clinton took the oath of office Wednesday and then
> spoke to America briefly, forcefully, and from deep in his heart. It is a
> matter of no small interest that Clinton wrote his own inaugural ad-
> dress. . . . A speechwriter might have turned more eloquent or memora-
> ble phrases, but they would have been, after all, the product of the writer,
> not the president. (January 21, 1993).

Dan Balz of the *Washington Post* praised the speech, saying:

> It was short—14 minutes almost to the second—and crisply delivered
> with a fresh cadence rarely achieved in his other major speeches. . . . The
> inaugural speech yesterday seemed authentic Clinton, distilled from cam-
> paign rhetoric of a dizzying year and repackaged for the inauguration,
> when unity and solemnity are the order of the day, when realism merges
> with optimism. (January 21, 1993, p. 1)

Wall Street Journal writers Jeffrey H. Birnbaum and Michael K. Frisby described the occasion:

... In a ceremony that represented not just a passing of the torch from one president to another, but also the passage of power from one generation to the next, the 46-year-old Mr. Clinton appealed directly to his fellow baby-boomers to accept responsibility for their government. ... Speaking without an overcoat with the temperature in the 40s, Mr. Clinton subtly evoked the memory of two leaders who shaped the political consciousness of his generation: John F. Kennedy and Martin Luther King, Jr. (January 21, 1993, p. A16)

President Clinton's speech: My fellow citizens, today we celebrate the mystery of American renewal. This ceremony is held in the depth of winter, but by the words we speak and the faces we show the world, we force the spring. A spring reborn in the world's oldest democracy that brings forth the vision and courage to reinvent America.

When our founders boldly declared America's independence to the world and our purposes to the Almighty, they knew that America to endure would have to change. Not change for change sake but change to preserve America's ideals—life, liberty, the pursuit of happiness. Though we march to the music of our time, our mission is timeless. Each generation of Americans must define what it means to be an American.

On behalf of our nation, I salute my predecessor, President Bush, for his half-century of service to America.

And I thank the millions of men and women whose steadfastness and sacrifice triumphed over depression, fascism, and communism. Today, a generation raised in the shadows of the cold war assumes new responsibilities in a world warmed by the sunshine of freedom but threatened still by ancient hatreds and new plagues.

Raised in unrivaled prosperity, we inherit an economy that is still the world's strongest but is weakened by business failures, stagnant wages, increasing inequality, and deep divisions among our own people.

When George Washington first took the oath I have just sworn to uphold, news traveled slowly across the land by horseback and across the ocean by boat. Now the sights and sounds of this ceremony are broadcast instantaneously to billions around the world. Communications and commerce are global, investment is mobile, technology is almost magical, and ambition for a better life is now universal. We earn our livelihood in America today in peaceful competition with people all across the earth. Profound and powerful forces are shaking and remaking the world. And the urgent question of our time is whether we can make change our friend and not our enemy.

This new world has already enriched the lives of millions of Americans who are able to compete and win in it. But when most people are working harder for less, when others cannot work at all, when the cost of health care devastates families and threatens to bankrupt our enterprises great and small, when the fear of crime robs law-abiding citizens of their freedom, and when millions of poor children cannot even imagine the lives we are calling them to lead, we have not made change our friend. We know we have to face hard truths and take strong steps, but we have not done so. Instead, we have drifted, and that drifting has eroded our resources, fractured our economy, and shaken our confidence.

Though our challenges are fearsome, so are our strengths. Americans have ever been a restless, questing, hopeful people, and we must bring to our task today the vision and will of those who came before us. From our Revolution to the Civil War, to the great depression, to the civil right's movement, our people have always mustered the determination to construct from these crises the pillars of our history.

Thomas Jefferson believed that to preserve the very foundations of our nation we would need dramatic change from time to time. Well my fellow Americans, this is our time. Let us embrace it.

Our democracy must be not only the envy of the world but the energy of our own renewal. There is nothing wrong with America that cannot be cured by what is right with America. And so today we pledge an end to the era of deadlock and drift, and a new season of American renewal has begun.

To renew America we must be bold. We must do what no generation has had to do before. We must invest more in our own people—in their jobs and in their future—and at the same time cut our massive debt. And we must do so in a world in which we must compete for every opportunity. It will not be easy. It will require sacrifice. But it can be done and done fairly. Not choosing sacrifice for its own sake, but for our sake. We must provide for our nation the way a family provides for its children.

Our founders saw themselves in that light of posterity. We can do no less. Anyone who has ever watched a child's eyes wander into sleep knows what posterity is. Posterity is the world to come, the world for whom we hold our ideals, from whom we have borrowed our planet and to whom we bear sacred responsibility. We must do what America does best: offer more opportunity to all and demand more responsibility from all.

It is time to break the bad habit of expecting something for nothing from our government and from each other. Let us all take more responsibility not only for ourselves and our families but for our communities and our country.

To renew America we must revitalize our democracy. This beautiful capital, like every capital since the dawn of civilization, is often a place of intrigue and calculation. Powerful people maneuver for position and worry endlessly about who is in and who is out, who is up and who is down, forgetting those people whose toil and sweat sends us here and pays our way.

Americans deserve better, and in this city there are people who want to do better. And so I say this to all of you here, let us resolve to reform our politics so that power and privilege no longer shout down the voice of the people. Let us put aside personal advantage so that we can feel the pain and see the promise of America. Let us resolve to make our government a place for what Franklin Roosevelt called bold, persistent experimentation, a government for our tomorrows, not our yesterdays. Let us give this capital back to the people to whom it belongs.

To renew America, we must meet challenges abroad as well as at home. There is no longer a clear division between what is foreign and what is domestic. The world economy, the world environment, the world AIDS crisis, the world arms race—they affect us all.

Today, as an old order passes, the new world is more free but less stable. Communism's collapse has called forth old animosities and new dangers. Clearly, America must continue to lead the world we did so much to make.

While America rebuilds at home, we will not shrink from the challenges nor fail to seize the opportunities of this new world. Together with our friends and allies we will work to shape change lest it engulf us. When our vital interests are challenged or the will and conscious of the international community is defied, we will act with peaceful diplomacy whenever possible, with force when necessary.

The brave Americans serving our nation today in the Persian Gulf and Somalia, and wherever else they stand, are testament to our resolve.

But our greatest strength is the power of our ideas, which are still new in many lands. Across the world we see them embraced and we rejoice. Our hopes, our hearts, our hands are with those on every continent who are building democracy and freedom. Their cause is America's cause.

The American people have summoned the change we celebrate today. You have raised your voices in an unmistakable chorus, you have cast your votes in historic numbers, and you have changed the face of Congress, the presidency, and the political process itself. Yes, you, my fellow Americans have forced the spring.

Now we must do the work the season demands. To that work I now turn with all the authority of my office. I ask the Congress to join with me. But no President, no Congress, no government can undertake this mission alone. My fellow Americans, you, too, must play your part in our renewal.

I challenge a new generation of young Americans to a sense of service; to act on your idealism by helping troubled children, keeping company with those in need, reconnecting our torn communities. There is so much to be done. Enough, indeed, of millions of others who are still young in spirit to give of themselves in service, too.

In serving, we recognize a simple but powerful truth: We need each other and we must care for one another. Today we do more than celebrate America, we rededicate ourselves to the very idea of America: An idea born in revolution and renewed through two centuries of challenge; an idea tempered by the knowledge that but for fate we, the fortunate and the unfortunate, might have been each other; an idea ennobled by the faith that our nation can summon from its myriad diversity the deepest measure of unity; an idea infused with the conviction that America's long, heroic journey must go forever upward.

And so, my fellow Americans, as we stand at the edge of the twenty-first century, let us begin anew with energy and hope, with faith and discipline. And let us work until our work is done. The Scripture says, "And let us not be weary in well-doing, for in due season we shall reap if we faint not."

From this joyful mountaintop of celebration we hear a call to service in the valley. We have heard the trumpets, we have changed from guard. And now each in our own way, and with God's help, we must answer the call.

Thank you, and God bless you all.

FAREWELL ADDRESS: AMERICAN INTERVENTION[1]
George H. W. Bush[2]

A tradition dating back to George Washington is the delivery of a farewell address by a departing American president. To this day, Washington's farewell address is still read at the House of Representatives each year on his birthday. Although for many years the farewell address took the form of a written message sent by the president to the Congress, presidents since Woodrow Wilson have delivered their farewells directly to Congress, or in more recent years, to the nation via radio and television. The presidential farewells typically cite the accomplishments of the administration, warn of continuing or forthcoming problems, and often suggest guidelines for future courses of action.

As his term of office neared its end, George Bush decided not to deliver a traditional farewell address. Although he had been urged by aides to make a nationally televised address, he chose instead to give two last "farewell" addresses: one on December 15, 1992 at Texas A. & M. University, in College Station, Texas, where the Bush presidential library will be built; and the other on January 5, 1993 at the United States Military Academy, in West Point, New York. Both speeches focussed on foreign policy.

The speech given in West Point has been chosen for inclusion for two reasons: it was generally better received and more highly publicized than the speech given in College Station, and it was Mr. Bush's final speech as president.

Commenting on Mr. Bush's speech in West Point, Michael Wines noted:

No President since Lyndon B. Johnson has used military power as widely and as often as Mr. Bush, and his address today could easily be read as the rationale for that record—including wars in the Persian Gulf and Panama, and the current intervention on humanitarian grounds in Somalia. . . . Today, Mr. Bush offered his principles for the use of force. Some were simple common sense, like admonitions to intervene only when the stakes warrant it, and when no other policies work. But others

[1]Delivered in Eisenhower Hall, at the United States Military Academy, West Point, New York, at 1:20 P.M. on January 5, 1993.
[2]For biographical note, see Appendix.

lay at the core of the President's decisions to commit troops or aircraft to Panama, the Persian Gulf and Somalia, and to withhold them, so far, from the Bosnian war. (*New York Times*, January 6, 1993, p. 1)

Bush delivered the speech to 4,000 cadets of the United States Military Academy in West Point, N.Y., at 1:20 P.M. Although his speech was uninterrupted by applause, the President was warmly welcomed with cheers and thousands of waving white napkins as he and Mrs. Bush joined the cadets for lunch at Eisenhower Hall earlier in the day. At the end of the speech, the President was further applauded when he, as commander-in-chief, granted amnesty for all demerits to the Corps of Cadets.

James Gerstenzang noted that:

The President turned emotional when he spoke of "a quality of caring and kindness" that American troops have brought to their mission. His voice choking as he fought to keep his composure, Bush told of his visit five days ago to U.S. troops in Somalia. (*Los Angeles Times*, January 6, 1993, p. 1).

Michael Wines also noted that at one point the "President's voice broke as he spoke of the compassion of American troops in Somalia," recalling "the young marine, eyes filled with tears, holding the fragile arm of an emaciated child."

George Bush's speech: Thank you all very much. Good Luck. Please be seated. Thank you, General Graves, for that very kind introduction. Barbara and I are just delighted to be here and honored that we could be joined by our able Secretary of the Army Mike Stone. Of course, the man well-known here that heads our army, General Sullivan, General Gordon Sullivan and Gracie Graves, General Robert Foley, General Galloway; Shawn Daniel, well-known to everyone here—has been our host, in a sense; and a West Point alum who has been at my side for four years, out here somewhere, General Scowcroft, graduate of this great institution who served his country with such distinction. May I salute the members of the Board of Visitors. I see another I have to single out, General Galvin, save the best for last, the corps of cadets. Thank you for that welcome.

Let me begin with the hard part; it is difficult for a Navy person to come up to West Point after that game a month ago. Go ahead, rub it in. But I watched it. Amazing things can happen in sports. Look at the Oilers, my other team that took it in the chin the other day. But I guess the moral of all of this is that losing is never easy; trust me, I know something about that. But if you have to lose, that's the way to do it. Fight with all you have. Give it your best shot. And win or lose, learn from it, and get on with life.

And I am about to get on with the rest of my life. But before I do, I want to share with you at this institution of leadership some of my thinking, both about the world you will soon be called upon to enter and the life you have chosen.

Any President has several functions. He speaks for and to the nation. He must faithfully execute the law. And he must lead. But no function, none of the President's hats, in my view, is more important than his role as Commander-in-Chief. For it is as Commander-in-Chief that the President confronts and makes decisions that one way or another affects the lives of everyone in this country as well as many others around the world.

I have had many occasions to don this most important of hats. Over the past four years, the men and women who proudly and bravely wear the uniforms of the U.S. armed services have been called upon to go in harm's way, and have discharged their duty with honor and professionalism.

I wish I could say that such demands were a thing of the past, that with the end of the Cold War the calls upon the United States would diminish. I cannot. Yes, the end of the Cold War, we would all concede, is a great blessing. It is a time of great promise. Democratic governments have never been so numerous. What happened two or three days ago in Moscow would not have been possible in the Cold War days. Thanks to historic treaties, such as that START II pact just reached with Russia, the likelihood of nuclear holocaust is vastly diminished.

But this does not mean that there is no specter of war, no threats to be reckoned with. And already, we see disturbing signs of what this new world could become if we are passive and aloof. We would risk the emergence of a world characterized by violence, characterized by chaos, one in which dictators and tyrants threaten their neighbors, build arsenals brimming with weapons of mass destruction, and ignore the welfare of their own men, women and children. And we could see a horrible increase in international terrorism, with American citizens more at risk than ever before.

We cannot and need not allow this to happen. Our objective must be to exploit the unparalleled opportunity presented by the Cold War's end: to work toward transforming this new world into a new world order, one of governments that are democratic, tolerant, and economically free at home, and committed abroad to settling inevitable differences peacefully, without the threat or use of force.

Unfortunately, not everyone subscribes to these principles. We continue to see leaders bent on denying fundamental human rights and seizing territory regardless of the human cost. No, an international society, one more attuned to the enduring principles that have made this country a beacon of hope for so many for so long, will not just emerge on its own. It's got to be built.

Two hundred years ago, another departing President warned of the dangers of what he described as "entangling alliances." His was the right course for a new nation at that point in history. But what was "entangling" in Washington's day is now essential. This is why, at Texas A&M a few weeks ago, I spoke of the folly of isolationism and of the importance—morally, economically, and strategically—of the United States remaining involved in world affairs. We must engage ourselves if a new world order—one more compatible with our values and congenial to our interest—is to emerge. But even more, we must lead.

Leadership, well, it takes many forms. It can be political or diplomatic, it can be economic or military, it can be moral or spiritual leadership. Leadership can take any one of these forms, or it can be a combination of them.

Leadership should not be confused with either unilateralism or universalism. We need not respond by ourselves to each and every outrage of violence. The fact that America can act does not mean that it must. A nation's sense of idealism need not be at odds with its interests, nor does principle replace prudence.

No, the United States should not seek to be the world's policeman. There is no support abroad or at home for us to play this role, nor should there be. We would exhaust ourselves, in the process wasting precious resources needed to address those problems at home and abroad that we cannot afford to ignore.

But in the wake of the Cold War, in a world where we are the only remaining superpower, it is the role of the United States to marshal its moral and material resources to promote a democratic peace. It is our responsibility—it is our opportunity—to lead. There is no one else.

Leadership cannot be simply asserted or demanded; it must be demonstrated. Leadership requires formulating worthy goals, persuading others of their virtue, and contributing one's share of the common effort and then some. Leadership takes time, it takes patience, it takes work.

Some of this work must take place here at home. Congress does have a constitutional role to play. Leadership therefore also invokes working with the Congress, and the American people, to provide the essential domestic underpinning if U.S. military commitments are to be sustainable.

This is what our administration, the Bush administration has tried to do. When Saddam Hussein invaded Kuwait, it was the United States that galvanized the U.N. Security Council to act and then mobilized the successful coalition on the battlefield. The pattern, not exactly the same but similar, in Somalia: first the United States underscored the importance of alleviating a growing tragedy, and then we organized humanitarian efforts designed to bring hope, food, and peace.

At times, real leadership requires a willingness to use military force. And force can be a useful backdrop to diplomacy, a complement to it, or, if need be, a temporary alternative.

As Commander-in-Chief, I have made the difficult choice to use military force. I determined we could not allow Saddam's forces to ravage Kuwait and hold this critical region at gunpoint. I thought then, and I think now, that using military force to implement the resolutions of the U.N. Security Council was in the interest of the United States and the world community. The need to use force arose as well in the wake of the Gulf War, when we came to the aid of the peoples of both northern and southern Iraq. And more recently, as I'm sure you know, I determined that only the use of force could stem this human tragedy of Somalia.

The United States should not stand by with so many lives at stake, and when a limited deployment of U.S. forces, buttressed by the forces of other countries and acting under the full authority of the United Nations, could make an immediate and dramatic difference—and do so without excessive levels of risk and cost— Operations Provide Comfort and Southern Watch in Iraq, and then Operation Restore Hope in Somalia, all bear witness to the wisdom of selected use of force for selective purposes.

Sometimes the decision not to use force—to stay our hand—I can tell you, it's just as difficult as the decision to send our soldiers into battle. The former Yugoslavia, well, it's been such a situation. There are, we all know, important humanitarian and strategic interests at stake there. But up to now it's not been clear that the application of limited amounts of force by the United States and its traditional friends and allies would have had the desired effect given the nature and complexity of that situation.

Our assessment of the situation in the former Yugoslavia could well change if and as the situation changes. The stakes could grow, the conflict could threaten to spread. Indeed, we are constantly reassessing our options, and are actively consulting with others about steps that might be taken to contain the fighting, protect the humanitarian effort, and deny Serbia the fruits of aggression.

Military force is never a tool to be used lightly or universally. In some circumstances it may be essential, in others counterproductive. I know that many people would like to find some formula—some easy formula to apply—to tell us with precision when and where to intervene with force. Anyone looking for scientific certitude is in for a disappointment. In the complex new world we are entering, there can be no single or simple set of fixed rules for using force. Inevitably, the question of military intervention requires judgment; each and every case is unique. To adopt rigid criteria would guarantee mistakes involving American interests and American lives. And it would give would-be troublemakers a blueprint for determining their own actions. It could signal U.S. friends and allies that our support was not to be counted on.

Similarly, we cannot always decide in advance which interests will require our using military force to protect them. The relative importance of an interest is not a guide: military force may not be the best way of safeguarding something vital, while using force might be the best way to protect an interest that qualifies as important but less than vital.

But to warn against a futile quest for a set of hard and fast rules to govern the use of military force is not to say there cannot be some principles to inform our decisions. Such guidelines can prove useful in sizing and, indeed, shaping our forces and in helping us to think our way through this key question.

Using military force makes sense as a policy where the stakes warrant; where and when force can be effective; where no other policies are likely to prove effective; where its application can be limited in scope and time; and where the potential benefits justify the potential costs and sacrifice.

Once we are satisfied that force makes sense, we must act with the maximum possible support. The United States can and should lead, but we will want to act in concert, where possible, involving the United Nations or other multinational grouping.

The United States can and should contribute to the common undertaking in a manner commensurate with our wealth, with our strength. But others should also contribute militarily, be it by providing combat or support forces, access to facilities or bases, or overflight rights. And similarly, others should contribute economically. It is unreasonable to expect the United States to bear the full financial burden of intervention when other nations have a stake in the outcome.

A desire for international support must not become a prerequisite for acting, though. Sometimes, a great power has to act alone. I made a tough decision—I might say, on advice of our outstanding military leaders who are so well known to everybody here—to use military force in Panama, when American lives and the security of the canal appeared to be threatened by outlaws who stole power in the face of free elections. And similarly, we moved swiftly to safeguard democracy in the Philippines.

But in every case involving the use of force, it will be essential to have a clear and achievable mission; a realistic plan for accomplishing the mission; and criteria no less realistic for withdrawing U.S. forces once the mission is complete. Only if we keep these principles in mind will the potential sacrifice be one that can be explained and justified. We must never forget that using force is not some political abstraction, but a real commitment of our fathers and mothers, and sons and daughters, brothers and sisters, friends and neighbors. You've got to look at it in human terms.

In order even to have the choice, we must have available adequate military forces tailored for a wide range of contingencies, including peacekeeping. Indeed, leading the effort toward a new world order will require a modern, capable military, in some areas necessitating more rather than less defense spending. As President, I have said that my ability to deploy force on behalf of U.S. interests abroad, made possible because past presidents—and I would single out in particular, my predecessor Ronald Reagan—and past secretaries of defense, sustained a strong military. Consistent with this sacred trust, I am proud to pass on to my successor, President-elect Clinton, a military second to none. We have the very best.

And, yet, it is essential to recognize that as important as such factors are, any military is more than simply the sum of its weapons or the state of its technology. What makes any armed force truly effective is the quality of its leadership, the quality of its training, the quality of its people.

We have succeeded abroad in no small part because of our people in uniform. The men and women in our Armed Forces have demonstrated their ability to master the challenges of modern warfare. And at the same time, and whether on the battlefield of Iraq or in some tiny village in Somalia, America's soldiers have always brought a quality of caring and kindness to their mission. Who will ever forget—I know I won't—those terrified Iraq soldiers surrendering to American troops? And who will forget the way the American soldier held out his arms and said, "It's okay. You're all right now." Or in Somalia, the young Marine, eyes filled with tears, holding the fragile arm of an emaciated child. There can be no doubt about it: the all volunteer force is one of the true success stories of modern day America.

It is instructive to look at just why this is so. At its heart, a voluntary military is based upon choice—you all know that—the decision taken freely by young men and women to join, the decision by mature men and women to remain. And the institution of the armed forces has thrived on its commitment to developing and promoting excellence. It is meritocracy in action. Race, religion, wealth, background count not. Indeed, the military offers many examples for the rest of society, showing what can be done to eradicate the scourge of drugs, to break down the barriers of racial discrimination, to offer equal opportunity to women.

This is not just a result of self-selection. It also reflects the military's commitment to education and training. You know, people speak of defense conversion, the process by which the defense firms re-tool for civilian tasks. Well, defense conversion within the military has been going on for years. It is the constant process of training and retraining, which the military does so well, that allows individuals to keep up with the latest technology, take on more challenging assignments, and prepare for life on the outside.

Out of this culture of merit and competition have emerged hundreds of thousands of highly skilled men and women brimming with real self-confidence. What they possess is a special mix of discipline, a willingness to accept direction, and the confidence—a willingness to accept responsibility. Together, discipline and confidence provide the basis for winning, for getting the job done.

There is no higher calling, no more honorable choice than the one that you here today have made. To join the armed forces is to be prepared to make the ultimate sacrifice for your country and for your fellow man.

What you have done, what you are doing, sends an important message, one that I feel sometimes gets lost amidst today's often materialist, self-interested culture. It is important to remember, it is important to demonstrate, that there is a higher purpose to life beyond one's self. Now, I speak of family, of community, of ideals. I speak of duty, honor, country.

There are many forms of contributing to this country, of public service. Yes, there is government. There is volunteerism—I love to talk about the thousand points of light, one American helping another—the daily tasks that require doing in our classrooms, in our hospitals, our cities, our farms. All can and do represent a form of service. In whatever form, service benefits our society and it enobles the giver. It is a cherished American concept, one we should continue to practice and pass on to our children.

This is what I wanted to share on this occasion. You are beginning your service to country; and I am nearing the end of mine. In exactly half a century ago, in June of 1942, as General Graves mentioned, we were at war, and I was graduating from school. The speaker that day at Andover was the then-Secretary of War, Henry Stimson. And his message was one of public service, but with a twist, on the importance of finishing one's schooling before going off to fight for one's country.

I listened closely to what he had to say, but I didn't take his advice. And that day was my eighteenth birthday. And when the commencement ceremony ended, I went on into Boston, and enlisted in the Navy as a seaman second class. And I never regretted it. You, too, have signed up. You, too, will never regret it. And I salute you for it.

Fortunately, because of the sacrifices made in years before me and still being made, you should be able to complete this phase of your education. A half century has passed since I left school to go into the service; a half century has passed since that day when Stimson spoke of the challenge of creating a new world.

You will also be entering a new world, one far better than the one I came to know, a world with the potential to be far better yet. This is the challenge, this is the opportunity of your lifetimes. I envy you for it, and I wish you Godspeed.

And while I'm at it, as your Commander-in-Chief, I hereby

grant amnesty to the Corps of Cadets. Thank you all very much. Thank you. Thank you very, very much. Good luck to all of you. Warm up here. Good luck to you guys. Thank you.

STATE OF THE UNION ADDRESS[1]
William J. Clinton[2]

A newly elected president begins the term with two major speeches: the inaugural address, which serves as a symbol of transition and sets the tone of the new administration; and the state of the union address.

After twelve years of Republican occupancy of the White House, public interest in the first two speeches of the new Democratic president was high. Clinton's swearing in and the deliverance of his inaugural address occurred on January 20, 1993. It wasn't until February 17 that Clinton, in his state of the Union address, revealed the specific proposals and plans of his administration. Since Clinton's campaign rested primarily on a platform of economic improvement, it was not surprising that his state of the union address also concentrated on economic issues. Two *Washington Post* reporters described the speech, stating:

The Clinton address, and the budget documents put out by his team yesterday, amount to the president's official transition from campaigning to governing. To get there, he was forced to put aside some prominent promises: to cut taxes on the middle class, to halve the deficit in four years, to provide increased health care for Americans with health cost controls. (Ruth Marcus and Ann Devroy, February 18, 1993, p. A1.)

President Clinton's particular care in preparation of his address suggests the importance that he attached to this speech. Gwen Ifill, of the *New York Times* reported that on the night before the address, the President summoned his top aides along with their deputies to the White House for a series of political and budget briefings. Ms. Ifill also reported that less than an hour before he was to deliver the speech, Mr. Clinton was still working on the text. Richard L. Berke remarks on Clinton's style of speech

---

[1]Delivered to a joint session of Congress, held in the House of Representatives, Washington, D.C., at 9:00 P.M. on February 17, 1993.
[2]For biographical note, see Appendix.

preparation, stating that "he likes to write, and rewrite, and rewrite speeches until the moment before he delivers them." Berke further notes that Clinton was unaware of the noon deadline to get the speech to the printers so it could be published and bound. Clinton missed the deadline and, as a result, the speech had to be duplicated on copying machines. "As his speech writers stood by in frustration," Berke comments, "Mr. Clinton reviewed the draft line by line, scrawling last minute fixes in the margins in his illegible handwriting. He also thought out loud the passages he wanted in the speech as his aides scribbled every word." (*New York Times*, February 18, 1993, p. A11.)

President Clinton delivered the speech to a nationally televised joint session of Congress in the House of Representatives at 9:00 P.M. Critical response to the speech was generally favorable as indicated by the following statements:

Anna Quindlen noted that, ". . . his state of the union address on the economy was about as good a speech I have ever heard him deliver." (*New York Times*, February 21, 1993, p. 17.)

William Raspberry remarked, "I liked the shape and feel of the address to Congress. It may have been the best speech Clinton ever delivered (and the best Clinton ever delivered a speech.)" (*The Advocate*, Baton Rouge, Louisiana, February 25, 1993, p. 6B.)

Leslie H. Gelb: "This column is to praise President Clinton for his stunningly honest and realistic economic speech last week and to point out that leaders abroad are hailing it left and right." (*New York Times*, February 21, 1993, p. A14.)

Mitchell Locin and Michael Arndt: "Using a conversational, chatty style, and a clear command of the often arcane elements of fiscal planning, Clinton unfurled a blueprint for his presidency. The speech before a joint session of Congress ran one hour and repeatedly brought wildly cheering Democrats to their feet." (*Chicago Tribune*, February 18, 1993, p. 1.)

New York Times editorial: "All President Clinton promised was an economic plan, but his speech to Congress offered something even rarer along the marshy rim of the Potomac—a vision." (February 19, 1993, p. A14.)

Ellen Goodman: "For the first time in years, a president delivered a speech without reaching into that small generic stash of heroes to sweeten the message. There were no pretty phrases in his hour-long economic lecture, no mornings in America, no eloquence to stir the goose-bumps." (*The Advocate*, Baton Rouge, Louisiana, February 22, 1993, p. 8B.)

According to James Adams, "Immediately after his State of

the Union speech, polls showed that Clinton was getting an 80% approval rating across the country, a reflection of a performance that had power and conviction." (*Sunday Times*, London, February 21, 1993, p. 16.) The *Chicago Tribune* also reported that polls taken after the speech indicated that people were willing to answer the call to sacrifice by paying higher taxes if the revenues were used to reduce the deficit. (February 18, 1993.)

President Clinton's speech: Mr. President, Mr. Speaker: When Presidents speak to the Congress and the nation from this podium, they typically comment on the full range of challenges and opportunities that face us. But these are not ordinary times. For all the many tasks that require our attention, one calls on us to focus, unite and act. Together, we must make our economy thrive once again.

It has been too long—at least three decades—since a President has challenged Americans to join him on our great national journey, not merely to consume the bounty of today but to invest for a much greater one tomorrow.

Nations, like individuals, must ultimately decide how they wish to conduct themselves, how they wish to be thought of by those with whom they live, and, later, how they wish to be judged by history. Like every man and woman, they must decide whether they are prepared to rise to the occasions history presents them.

We have always been a people of youthful energy and daring spirit. And at this historic moment, as Communism has fallen, as freedom is spreading around the world, as a global economy is taking shape before our eyes, Americans have called for change, and now it is up to those of us in this room to deliver.

Our nation needs a new direction. Tonight, I present to you our comprehensive plan to set our nation on that new course.

I believe we will find our new direction in the basic values that brought us here: opportunity, individual responsibility, community, work, family and faith. We need to break the old habits of both political parties in Washington. We must say that there can be no more something for nothing, and we are all in this together.

The conditions which brought us to this point are well known. Two decades of low productivity and stagnant wages; persistent unemployment and underemployment; years of huge government deficits and declining investment in our future; exploding health care costs, and lack of coverage; legions of poor children; educational and job training opportunities inadequate to the demands of a high wage, high growth economy. For too long we drifted without a strong sense of purpose, responsibility or community, and our political system too often was paralyzed by special interest groups, partisan bickering and the sheer complexity of our problems.

I know we can do better, because ours remains the greatest nation on earth, the world's strongest economy and the world's only military superpower. If we have the vision, the will and the heart to make the changes we must, we will enter the 21st century with possibilities our parents could not even have imagined, having secured the American dream for ourselves and future generations.

I well remember, 12 years ago Ronald Reagan stood at this podium and told the American people that if our debt were stacked in dollar bills, the stack would reach 67 miles into space. Today, that stack would reach 267 miles.

I tell you this not to assign blame for this problem. There is plenty of blame to go around, in both branches of the Government and both parties. The time for blame has come to an end. I came here to accept responsibility; I want you to accept responsibility for the future of this country, and if we do it right, I don't care who gets the credit for it.

Our plan has four fundamental components:

First, it reverses our economic decline, by jump-starting the economy in the short term and investing in our people, their jobs and their incomes in the long term.

Second, it changes the rhetoric of the past into the actions of the present, by honoring work and families in every part of our lives.

Third, it substantially reduces the Federal deficit, honestly and credibly.

Finally, it earns the trust of the American people by paying for these plans first with cuts in Government waste and inefficiency— cuts, not gimmicks, in Government spending—and by fairness, for a change, in the way the burden is borne.

Tonight, I want to talk about what government can do, because I believe our government must do more for the hardworking people who pay its way. But let me say first: government cannot do this alone. The private sector is the engine of economic growth in America. And every one of us can be an engine of change in our own lives. We've got to give people more opportunity, but we must also demand more responsibility in return.

Our immediate priority is to create jobs, now. Some say we're in a recovery. Well, we all hope so. But we're simply not creating jobs. And there is no recovery worth its salt that does not begin with new jobs.

To create jobs and guarantee a strong recovery, I call on Congress to enact an immediate jobs package of over $30 billion. We will put people to work right now and create half a million jobs: jobs that will rebuild our highways and airports, renovate housing, bring new life to our rural towns and spread hope and opportunity among our nation's youth with almost 700,000 jobs for them this summer alone. And I invite America's business leaders to join us in this effort, so that together we can create a million summer jobs in cities and poor rural areas for our young people.

Second, our plan looks beyond today's business cycle, because our aspirations extend into the next century. The heart of our plan deals with the long term. It has an investment program designed to increase public and private investment in areas critical to our economic future. And it has a deficit reduction program that will increase savings available for private sector investment, lower interest rates, decrease the percentage of the Federal budget claimed by interest payments, and decrease the risk of financial market disruptions that could adversely affect the economy.

Over the long run, all this should result in a higher rate of economic growth, improved productivity, higher wages, more high-quality jobs and an improved economic competitive position in the global economy.

In order to accomplish public investment and deficit reduction, Government spending is being cut and taxes are being increased. Our spending cuts were carefully thought through to try to minimize any economic impact, to capture the peace dividend for investment purposes and to switch the balance in the budget from consumption to investment. The tax increases and spending cuts were both designed to assure that the cost of this historic program to face and deal with our problems is borne by those who could most readily afford that cost.

Our plan is designed to improve the health of American business through lower interest rates, improved infrastructure, better trained workers, and a stronger middle class. Because small businesses generate most of our nation's jobs, our plan includes the boldest targeted incentives for small business in history. We propose a permanent investment tax credit for small business, and new rewards for entrepreneurs who take risks. We will give small business access to the brilliant technologies of our time and to the credit they need to prosper and flourish.

With a new network of community development banks, and one billion dollars to make the dream of enterprise zones real, we will begin to bring new hope and new jobs to storefronts and factories from South Boston to South Texas to South-Central Los Angeles.

Our plan invests in our roads, bridges, transit facilities; in high-speed railways and high-tech information systems; and in the most ambitious environmental clean-up of our time.

On the edge of the new century, economic growth depends as never before on opening up new markets overseas. And so we will insist on fair trade rules in international markets.

A part of our national economic strategy must be to expand trade on fair terms, including successful completion of the latest round of world trade talks. A North American Free Trade Agreement with appropriate safeguards for workers and the environment. At the same time, we need an aggressive attempt to create the hi-tech jobs of the future; special attention to troubled industries like aerospace and airlines, and special assistance to displaced workers like those in our defense industry.

I pledge that business, government and labor will work together in a partnership to strengthen America for a change.

But all of our efforts to strengthen the economy will fail unless we take bold steps to reform our health care system. America's businesses will never be strong; America's families will never be secure; and America's government will never be solvent until we tackle our health care crisis.

The rising costs and the lack of care are endangering both our economy and our lives. Reducing health care costs will liberate hundreds of billions of dollars for investment and growth and new jobs. Over the long run, reforming health care is essential to reducing our deficit and expanding investment.

Later this spring, I will deliver to Congress a comprehensive plan for health care reform that will finally get costs under control. We will provide security to all our families, so that no one will be denied the coverage they need. We will root out fraud and outrageous charges, and make sure that paperwork no longer chokes you or your doctor. And we will maintain American standards, the highest quality medical care in the world and the choices we demand and deserve. The American people expect us to deal with health care. And we must deal with it now.

Perhaps the most fundamental change our new direction offers is its focus on the future and the investments we seek in our children.

Each day we delay carries a dear cost. Half our two-year-olds don't receive immunizations against deadly diseases. Our plan will provide them for every eligible child. And we'll save ten dollars for every one we'll spend by eliminating preventable childhood diseases.

The Women, Infants, and Children nutrition program will be expanded so that every expectant mother who needs our help receives it.

Head Start, a program that prepares children for school, is a success story. It saves money, but today it reaches only one-third of all eligible children. Under our plan, we will cover every eligible child. Investing in Head Start and WIC is not only the right thing, it's the smart thing. For every dollar we invest today, we save three tomorrow.

America must ask more of our students, our teachers, and our schools. And we must give them the resources they need to meet high standards.

We will bring together business and schools to establish new apprenticeships, and give young people the skills they need today to find productive jobs tomorrow.

Lifelong learning will benefit workers throughout their careers. We must create a new unified worker training system, so that workers receive training regardless of why they lost their jobs.

Our national service program will make college loans available to all Americans, and challenge them to give something back to their country, as teachers, police officers, community service workers. This will be an historic change on a scale with the creation of the Land Grant Colleges and the G.I. Bill. A hundred years from now, historians who owe their education to our plan for national service will salute your vision.

We believe in jobs, we believe in learning, and we believe in rewarding work. We believe in restoring the values that make America special.

There is dignity in all work, and there must be dignity for all workers. To those who heal our sick, care for our children, and do our most tiring and difficult jobs, our new direction makes this solemn commitment:

By expanding the Earned Income Tax Credit, we will make history: We will help reward work for millions of working poor Americans. Our new direction aims to realize a principle as powerful as it is simple: If you work full time, you should not be poor.

Later this year, we will offer a plan to end welfare as we know it. No one wants to change the welfare system as much as those who are trapped by the welfare system.

We will offer people on welfare the education, training, child care and health care they need to get back on their feet. Then, after two years, they must get back to work—in private business if possible; in public service, if necessary. It's time to end welfare as a way of life.

Our next great goal is to strengthen American families.

We'll ask fathers and mothers to take more responsibility for their children. And we'll crack down on deadbeat parents who won't pay their child support.

We want to protect our families against violent crime which terrorizes our people and tears apart our communities. We must pass a tough crime bill. We need to put 100,000 more police on the street, provide boot camps for first-time non-violent offenders, and put hardened criminals behind bars. We have a duty to keep guns out of the hands of criminals. If you pass the Brady Bill, I'll sign it.

To make government work for middleclass taxpayers and not the special interests, we must reform our political system.

I'm asking Congress to enact real campaign finance reform. Let's reduce the power of special interests and increase the participation of the people. We should end the tax deduction for special interest lobbying and use the money to help clean up the political system. And we should quickly enact legislation to force lobbyists to disclose their activities.

But to revolutionize government we have to insure that it lives within its means. And that starts at the top, with the White House. In the last few weeks, I have cut the White House staff by twenty-five percent, saving ten million dollars. I ordered administrative cuts in the budgets of agencies and departments, I cut the federal bureaucracy by 100,000 positions, for combined savings of nine billion dollars. It's time for government to be as frugal as any household in America. That's why I congratulate the Congress for taking similar steps to cut its costs today. Together, we can show the American people that we have heard their call for change.

But we can go further. Tonight, I call for an across-the-board freeze in federal government salaries for one year. Thereafter, federal salaries will rise at a rate lower than the rate of inflation.

We must reinvent government to make it work again. We'll

push innovative education reform to improve learning, not just spend more money. We'll use the Superfund to clean up pollution, not just increase lawyers' incomes. We'll use federal banking regulators, not just to protect the security and safety of our financial institutions, but to break the credit crunch. And we'll change the whole focus of our poverty programs from entitlement to empowerment.

For years, there has been a lot of talk about the deficit, but very few credible efforts to deal with it. This plan does. Our plan tackles the budget deficit, seriously and over the long term. We will put in place one of the biggest deficit reductions and the biggest change of federal priorities in our history at the same time.

We are not cutting the deficit because the experts tell us to do so. We are cutting the deficit so that your family can afford a college education for your children. We are cutting the deficit so that your children will someday be able to buy a home of their own. We are cutting the deficit so that your company can invest in retraining its workers and retooling its factories. We are cutting the deficit so that government can make the investments that help us become stronger and smarter and safer.

If we do not act now, we will not recognize this country ten years from now. Ten years from now, the deficit will have grown to 635 billion dollars a year; the national debt will be almost 80 percent of our gross domestic product. Paying the interest on that debt will be the costliest government program of all, and we will continue to be the world's largest debtor, depending on foreign funds for a large part of our nation's investments.

Our budget will, by 1997, cut 140 billion dollars from the deficit, one of the greatest real spending cuts by an American president. We are making more than 150 difficult, painful reductions which will cut federal spending by 246 billion dollars. We are eliminating programs that are no longer needed, such as nuclear power research and development. We are slashing subsidies and cancelling wasteful projects. Many of these programs were justified in their time. But if we're going to start new plans, we must eliminate old ones. Government has been good at building programs, now we must show that we can limit them.

As we restructure American military forces to meet the new threats of the post-Cold War world, we can responsibly reduce our defense budget. But let no one be in any doubt: The men and women who serve under the American flag will be the best trained, best equipped, best prepared fighting force in the world, so long as I am President.

Backed by a leaner and more effective national defense and a stronger economy, our nation will be prepared to lead a world challenged by ethnic conflict, the proliferation of weapons of mass destruction, the global democratic revolution, and the health of our environment.

Our economic plan is ambitious, but it is necessary for the continued greatness of our country. And it will be paid for fairly, by cutting government, by asking the most of those who benefitted most in the past, by asking more Americans to contribute today so that all Americans can do better tomorrow.

For the wealthiest, those earning more than 180,000 dollars per year, I ask you to raise the top rate for federal income taxes from 31 percent to 36 percent. Our plan recommends a ten percent surtax on incomes over 250,000 dollars a year. And we will close the loopholes that let some get away without paying any tax at all.

For businesses with taxable incomes over ten million dollars, we will raise the corporate tax rate to 36 percent. And we will cut the deduction for business entertainment.

Our plan attacks tax subsidies that reward companies that ship jobs overseas. And we will ensure that, through effective tax enforcement, foreign corporations who make money in America pay the taxes they owe to America.

Middle-class Americans should know: You're not going alone any more; you're not going first; and you're no longer going to pay more and get less. Ninety-eight point eight percent of America's families will have no increase in their income tax rates. Only the wealthiest one point two percent will see their rates rise.

Let me be clear: There will be no new cuts in benefits from Medicare for beneficiaries. There will be cuts in payments to providers: doctors, hospitals, and labs, as a way of controlling health care costs. These cuts are only a stop-gap until we reform the whole health care system. Let me repeat that, because it matters to me, as I know it matters to you: This plan will not make new cuts in Medicare benefits for any beneficiary.

The only change we are making in Social Security is to ask those older Americans with higher incomes, who do not rely solely on Social Security to get by, to contribute more. This change will not affect eighty percent of Social Security recipients. If you do not pay taxes on Social Security now, you will not pay taxes on Social Security under this plan.

Our plan includes a tax on energy as the best way to provide us with new revenue to lower the deficit and invest in our people. Moreover, unlike other taxes, this one reduces pollution, increases energy efficiency, and eases our dependence on oil from unstable regions of the world.

Taken together, these measures will cost an American family earning 40 thousand dollars a year less than 17 dollars a month. And because of other programs we will propose, families earning less than 30,000 dollars a year will pay virtually no additional tax at all. Because of our publicly stated determination to reduce the deficit, interest rates have fallen since the election. That means that, for the middle class, the increases in energy costs will be more than offset by lower interest costs for mortgages, consumer loans and credit cards. This is a wise investment for you and for your country.

I ask all Americans to consider the cost of not changing, of not choosing a new direction. Unless we have the courage to start building our future and stop borrowing from it, we are condemning ourselves to years of stagnation, interrupted only by recession; to slow growth in jobs, no growth in incomes, and more debt and disappointment.

Worse yet, unless we change, unless we reduce the deficit, increase investment, and raise productivity so we can generate jobs—we will condemn our children and our children's children to a lesser life and a diminished destiny.

Tonight, the American people know we must change. But they are also likely to ask whether we have the fortitude to make those changes happen.

They know that, as soon as we leave this Chamber, the special interests will be out in force, trying to stop the changes we seek. The forces of conventional wisdom will offer a thousand reasons why it can't be done. And our people will be watching and wondering to see if it's going to be business as usual again.

So we must scale the walls of their skepticism, not with our words, but by our deeds. After so many years of gridlock and indecision, after so many hopeful beginnings and so few promising results, Americans will be harsh in their judgments of us if we fail to seize this moment.

This economic plan cannot please everybody. If this package is picked apart, there will be something that will anger each of us. But, if it is taken as a whole, it will help all of us.

Resist the temptation to focus only on a spending cut you don't like or some investment not made. And nobody likes tax increases. But let's face facts: For 20 years, incomes have stalled. For years, debt has exploded. We can no longer afford to deny reality. We must play the hand we were dealt.

The test of our program cannot simply be: What's in it for me? The question must be: What's in it for us?

If we work hard, and work together, if we rededicate ourselves to strengthening families, creating jobs, rewarding work, and reinventing government, we can lift America's fortunes once again.

Tonight I ask everyone in this Chamber, and every American, to look into their hearts, spark their hopes, and fire their imaginations. There is so much good, so much possibility, so much excitement in our nation. If we act boldly, as leaders should, our legacy will be one of progress and prosperity. This, then, is America's new direction. Let us summon the courage to seize the day.

Thank you very much. Good night. And may God bless America.

THE PRESIDENCY AND PUBLIC OPINION[1]
JOSEPH NOLAN[2]

Within days after Bill Clinton won the election, and long before his inauguration, friends, critics, supporters, and the media began advising the new chief executive on how he could best lead the country and implement the proposals that constitute his platform. Almost everyone—layman, politician, reporter, syndicated columnist—had an opinion. Not surprisingly, few people agreed on the proper course of action for the first Democratic president in twelve years.

One opinion was offered by Joseph Nolan, a journalist and scholar who had first become interested in the presidency and public opinion while he was a Washington correspondent for United Press International during the administration of Harry Truman. Nolan subsequently became a writer and editor at the

[1]Delivered to the Flagler Forum, Flagler College, St. Augustine, Florida, in the grand parlor of the Ponce de Leon Hotel, at 11:00 A.M. on November 19, 1992.
[2]For biographical note, see Appendix.

New York Times, completed a Ph.D. at New York University, and held positions as a professor of communications and public affairs at three major universities.

On November 19, 1992, just two weeks after the election, Dr. Nolan delivered a speech to the Flagler Forum, as part of the fall 1992 Continuing Education Program at Flagler College in St. Augustine, Florida. In the address, Nolan argued that in the just-completed campaign, all three contenders had courted public opinion more assiduously than ever before and predicted that in the future, presidential candidates would rely even more on popular television interview and talk shows for exposure.

Nolan delivered his address at 11:00 A.M. in the Grand Parlor of the historic Ponce de Leon hotel, now the main administration building of Flagler College. His audience consisted of about fifty adults, ranging from 50 to 70 years of age who were enrolled in the college's continuing education program. The speech received national attention when it was reprinted in *Vital Speeches of the Day.*

Joseph Nolan's speech: Let me say at the onset how much I admire both your tolerance and your stamina. For the past six months of the presidential campaign, the air has been filled with speeches—and vice versa. Yet you are still game for another one or two speeches here at the Flagler Forum.

David Brinkley was saying recently he's worried that we may be approaching the point where we have more people willing to make speeches than we have people willing to listen to them. I earnestly pray that we will not reach that fateful point this morning.

You may be surprised to hear an academic refer to prayer in view of all the fuss, during the political campaign, about prayer in the classroom. Let me assure you, though, that you need not worry. There will always be prayer in the classroom, as long as there are math exams.

Our topic this morning, "The Presidency and Public Opinion," is particularly timely, I think, because during the recent presidential campaign, all three contenders courted public opinion more assiduously than ever before. Not only did they use the traditional media outlets but for the first time they reached out to popular TV programs with millions of viewers: Larry King, Donahue, Oprah.

It worked. And I venture the prediction that by 1996, these shows will be interviewing not only the candidates themselves, but their doctors, their lawyers and even their shrinks.

My thesis is that how well President-elect Bill Clinton does in the next four years will depend decisively on how effectively he can mobilize public opinion behind his program for change.

Mr. Clinton moves into the Oval Office on January 20 with his party holding sizable majorities in both houses of Congress. He faces a nation clearly eager for action-oriented leadership. He will have an opportunity offered to only a handful of past presidents to set a new course for the nation. However, he can do this only if he is able to rally public opinion in support of his bold initiatives.

In a representative democracy such as ours, one of the prime qualifications of a President is that he can develop the skill to move the public toward consensus by playing a constructive role at every stage of the public opinion process: consciousness-raising, working through the need for change, and final resolution.

Regardless of what one may think of Ronald Reagan's presidency, he was extraordinarily adept at moving the nation towards consensus. He had a grand vision, whether you agreed with it or not. He was able to communicate that vision with unusual clarity. Above all, he could persuade the American people to follow his lead. And that's what President-elect Clinton must do if he is going to succeed.

Like any president, he starts with some formidable advantages. Americans traditionally root for a new president. They usually give him a "honeymoon period" to get his act together. The *Washington Post*'s famed editorial cartoonist Herblock, scourge of many a White House administration, boasts that he always gives an incoming President "one free shave" before sharpening his razor-like drawing pencil. Even the pollsters customarily hold off for a decent interval before posing their favorite "Do you approve or disapprove" questions.

Still the tides of public opinion can shift fast, so Mr. Clinton must move resolutely if he hopes to avoid the shoals that wrecked some of his White House predecessors.

To comprehend the increasingly vital link between the Presidency and public opinion, it is helpful to ask ourselves four key questions:

What is public opinion?

Why is it important to a president?

How well have presidents in the past succeeded in marshalling public opinion to their advantage?

What, specifically, must Mr. Clinton do to mobilize it behind his program for change?

Let's consider these questions one at a time, and see where we come out.

What is public opinion? Americans have been using this term since the late 18th century. Thomas Jefferson was one of the first to do so in enunciating the goal of basing American democracy on an informed public. Yet despite its familiarity, the term seems somehow remote, abstract, even a little mysterious. Pollsters try to measure it. Pundits attempt to interpret it. The press informs and influences it. And presidents worry about it, even when they are insisting they don't.

Over the years, a good many experts have taken a crack at defining public opinion, so it is no surprise, I suppose, that they haven't always agreed among themselves.

Mark Twain put his finger on one of the definitional difficulties, namely, separating privately held opinions from those that are publicly expressed. The author of *Tom Sawyer* and *Huckleberry Finn* said he made it a practice to expose to the world only his "trimmed and perfumed and carefully barbered public opinions." His private ones, he said, he concealed "carefully, cautiously and wisely."

I have always favored the succinct definition of the distinguished political scientist V. O. Key, Jr. Said Key, "Public opinion refers to those opinions held by private persons which governments find it prudent to heed." In other words, public opinion is a process of interactive communications between the people and their government. It is what results from ordinary folks speaking and reasoning together, on issues of common concern, in the traditional dialogue of democracy.

The American public, historically, has tended to be centrist, middle-of-the-road, rejecting extremism of the left or the right. The public is concerned mainly with results, rather than with the means of achieving them. It is generally inclined to accept the president's choice of means.

Public opinion can have a direct impact on presidential decisions, as it did on civil rights. But more often, it acts as a constraint on what is possible rather as an active promoter of a particular issue.

In recent years, it has driven two presidents from office: Lyndon Johnson over Vietnam and Richard Nixon over Watergate. In light of our latest election experience, some would add the name of George Bush to this list. After his stirring triumph in the Persian gulf war, he seemed unable to read and respond to public opinion that demanded similarly aggressive action here at home to get the nation out of recession. At a time when unemployment had touched one family in four, the impression grew that Mr. Bush neither understood nor cared about people's economic travail.

This was reflected in the polls. The President's approval rating dropped from 91 percent to the mid-30s within eighteen months—an unprecedented decline in the absence of a major scandal.

Mr. Bush and his aides blamed the media. But thoughtful analysis suggests that it was not so much the media that turned against him but public opinion. The media merely reported what happened. Over the last six months of the campaign, public opinion held remarkably steady. Three out of four people, according to the polls, disapproved of the way the President was handling the economy. It was just that simple. In the end, it is fair to say, Mr. Bush fell victim to our habit as a nation of asking too much of the men who hold our highest office.

Why is public opinion important to a president?

Senator Bill Bradley of New Jersey gave the best answer to that question. He said he was attending a political dinner in Washington one night when a waiter came around with the butter.

"I'd like two pats of butter, if I may, please," said Bradley.

"Sorry, buddy," said the waiter, "it's one to a customer."

"Well," said Bradley, "I guess you don't know who I am. I'm a senior member of the United States Senate. Before that, I was an All-Star basketball player with the New York Knicks. And before that, I was a Rhodes Scholar at Oxford."

The waiter was not impressed.

"I guess you don't know who I am," he retorted.

"No, I don't," said Bradley. "Who are you anyway?"

The waiter drew himself up to his full 5 feet 5 inches, and said proudly: "I'm the guy in charge of the butter."

That's the way it is in a democracy. Presidents have to pay attention to what people think because people are in charge of the butter.

We learn as children, in the third or fourth grade, that the highest political office in the land is important, and we develop feelings about the incumbent that tend to be overwhelmingly deferential and supportive. As long as the incumbent can maintain his supportive public opinion, he can pursue his goals with at least some hope of success.

Such support can help a president in several ways. It can bolster his confidence in his own program. It can strengthen him with cabinet officers who may be tempted to challenge him on a particular pet project. It can make members of Congress more willing to follow his lead, and less likely to attack his proposals if they feel he has strong support from the folks back home.

Indeed, it is no exaggeration to say that public opinion is a president's most vital constituency, shaping as it does his policies, his political future, even his eventual place in history.

The English author, statesman, and onetime ambassador to Washington, James Bryce, summed up the situation in memorable fashion. He wrote,

> Of all the experiments which America has made, this endeavoring to govern by public opinion is that which best deserves study. For her solution of the problem differs from all previous solutions, and she has shown more boldness in trusting public opinion, in recognizing and giving effect to it, than has yet been shown elsewhere . . . Public opinion stands out in the United States as the great source of power, the master of servants who tremble before it.

How well have presidents marshalled public opinion?

History suggests that those presidents, from Franklin D. Roosevelt to George Bush, who were most successful in getting their programs approved were the ones who effectively rallied public opinion behind their cause.

F. D. R. showed the way with his intimate "Fireside Chats." His compassionate conversations on the radio with a mass audience offered hope to a despairing nation during the Great Depression of the 1930s.

In their outreach efforts, F. D. R. and his successors have been able to draw upon impressive resources. They have access to the most up-to-date information banks, they have the most scientific and sophisticated polling techniques and facilities for monitoring the elusive pulse of democracy. And, above all, they have television which has provided the most powerful branch of government with the most effective medium of communications, whether for a primetime news conference or an urgent address to the nation.

Television is an intensely personal medium, and no person cuts so imposing a figure on the TV screen as the President himself. By reason of his office, he can summon the cameras of all the networks simultaneously, at a time and place of his own selection, to address a massive national audience.

What television and the press present is raw material on which the public forms its opinions, and presidents are keenly aware of this fact. I got some insight into it from one of my former graduate students at the University of South Carolina, Lee Atwater, who went on to become George Bush's 1988 campaign manager. One day over luncheon in Washington, I asked Lee about the impact of media over public policy.

He said: "Let me tell you something. In the time I was on the White House staff, I can't think of a single meeting that somebody didn't ask: 'How is this going to play in the media?' Major decisions were influenced all the time by media considerations. The impact of the media on public policy is enormous."

Recognizing this impact, modern presidents have tried to reach the public regularly through the White House news conference. This is an institution that dates back to Woodrow Wilson's administration. But it was not until Franklin D. Roosevelt moved into the White House that it really came into its own. F. D. R. used to meet with correspondents twice a week in spirited sessions in which he provided a running account of what he was doing and what he proposed to do. He was a master at simplifying the complexities of the nation's problems. He exulted in his own dramatic talents, once confiding to Orson Welles: "There are only two great actors in America, and you, Orson, are the other one."

The first White House news conference I covered was with Harry Truman on a day when he was his ornery, opinionated, outspoken self. I remember that one veteran correspondent got him riled up with a question to the effect that the Republican Congress did not feel he was treating them fairly.

"Don't you believe it," snapped Mr. Truman, "that charge is a lot of manure."

Not long afterward, one of Mrs. Truman's friends told her: "Bess, I do wish you could get Harry to stop saying 'manure.' It's just not presidential."

"My dear," sighed Bess Truman, "you should have heard what he was saying before I censored him."

Incidentally, if you have not had a chance to read David McCullough's affectionate biography, *Truman*, by all means add it to your holiday list. You'll readily see why both Mr. Bush and Mr. Clinton adopted him as their patron saint during the campaign.

It was Dwight Eisenhower who first opened the White House news conference to television cameras. He hedged a little, though, by reserving the right to edit out his tangled syntax before the tapes were used on the air.

John Kennedy, a news reporter and writer himself at one time, relished his give-and-take exchanges with correspondents, and made the news conferences lively events. By comparison, Lyndon Johnson was not nearly so skillful at fending off correspondents without offending them. Nor was Richard Nixon who often gave the impression that he felt most of the correspondents were out to get him.

Today, the White House news conference has come to occupy a prominent place in American political life. It is the only regular forum in which the nation can see the chief executive in an active interchange with people outside his administration. Some would like to improve it, but nobody wants to abandon it, least of all the Presidents who view it as an indispensable link to their most important constituency.

What must Mr. Clinton do to marshal public opinion? The short answer is that he must act promptly. And there are already signs that he realizes this. Any new president has only a short time to persuade people that he is fully capable of leading the nation. Much depends on what he does in the first three to six months. That's when he has a chance to define his mandate before the media and the opposition define it for him.

Some chief executives have been quick to seize the initiative. F. D. R. laid the groundwork for the New Deal's far-reaching social programs, fifteen laws in all, in his first three months. John Kennedy transformed his image from that of a "young," "pushy" outsider to a President of all the people. Lyndon Johnson steered through a balky Congress the historical civil rights legislation.

The test for Mr. Clinton will be how quickly he can convert his mandate into momentum. Having won public support, he must now persuade people that they have a powerful stake in what happens next. More specifically, in my view, he must:

Convey a convincing impression of boldness and change;

Recognize that his something-for-everybody campaign proposals were designed to appease prime voting blocs, and must now be screened for timeliness and merit;

Select a few, just a few, high-priority initiatives and single-mindedly push them through, realizing that any new President gets only a few of the things on his Wish List;

Get moving on a program to stimulate the economy, demonstrating the caring and commitment that many have found lacking in Mr. Bush's approach;

Be willing to say "no" to the special pleaders, even those interest groups that contributed mightily to his election victory;

Work to keep alive the passions and enthusiasm so evident in the campaign by reaching out to those who opposed him or sat on the sidelines, to build a new consensus in pursuit of common goals;

Begin talking candidly about the pain and sacrifice the nation must endure to get its economic house in order. For without candor on this pivotal issue he will have no creditability. And with creditability he risks losing the support of public opinion he has mustered up to this point.

In his first post-election news conference, Mr. Clinton said: "I have to do my best at one of the most important jobs of the President: to communicate to the American people exactly where we are at this point in our history, how we got here, and where we're going in the future."

He's right on the mark about his responsibility. Now, as today's college generation would say: "Mr. President, just do it!"

NEW DIRECTIONS IN FOREIGN RELATIONS

AMERICAN FOREIGN POLICY IN A NEW AGE[1]
WARREN CHRISTOPHER[2]

Two days after Boris Yeltsin called for a national referendum asking the Russian people to endorse his leadership and a new constitution and parliament, Warren Christopher delivered his first foreign policy speech as Secretary of State to an audience of business executives and government officials in Chicago.

In the address, Christopher described the Russian political crisis as the "greatest strategic challenge of our time." Asserting that the United States should not walk away from its role as a world leader, Christopher compared the current choice that America faces to two other twentieth-century watershed moments:

> We stand again at a historical crossroads. It is very reminiscent of the crossroads that we faced in 1918 and 1945. Then we were summoned after conflicts to lead the world by building a new peace. After World War I we chose to retreat, and the consequences were disastrous. However, after World War II, our leaders had the wisdom to answer the call.

Several reporters described Christopher's address as the start of the Clinton administration's campaign to persuade the American people to provide support for Yeltsin and his program, even if this support is in the form of substantial foreign aid to the Russians.

Mr. Christopher's address was sponsored by the Chicago Council on Foreign Relations, the Executive's Club of Chicago and the Mid-American Committee. All three groups regularly arrange for lectures to be given by prominent American and foreign government officials. Christopher delivered the address in Chicago's Fairmount Hotel, on March 22nd, 1993 to an audience estimated at between 800 and 1,000 people.

[1]Delivered at the Fairmount Hotel, Chicago, Illinois, at noon on March 22, 1993.

[2]For biographical note, see Appendix.

Although sworn in as Secretary of State just two months earlier, Christopher had been a senior advisor to the Clinton presidential campaign and coordinator of the transition between the Bush and Clinton administrations. Earlier, he had served as Deputy Secretary of State from 1977 to 1981 and as Deputy Attorney General from 1967 to 1969.

Steven Greenhouse, writing in the *New York Times,* described the Secretary's address as follows:

Mr. Christopher delivered his speech today in the subdued, nearly deadpan manner of the lawyer-turned-diplomat. But the language was unusually categorical for a secretary of state as he pledged stepped-up economic aid to Russia and tried to make a case for spending more money overseas.

Warren Christopher's speech: Ladies and gentlemen. It's a pleasure to be with you today. I'm especially happy to be speaking to this audience. Secretaries of State spend so much of their time explaining to foreign diplomats that they tend to take for granted the one audience that really counts, you, the American people.

I want to say a special welcome to the students that are here from the congressional districts of Congressmen Reynolds and Rush. You have a tremendous stake in our foreign policy. After all, you are the ones who will have to live with the consequences of our actions. So it's critical that your voice be heard. I am very glad you could join us today.

My trip here is only the first of many that I will be making to cities and towns across this country. My mission is simple: to begin an ongoing conversation with the American people about the new world we live in and our country's proper role in it.

It is fitting that I launch this process in Chicago. Yours is a city that in so many ways symbolizes America, by its location in our country's heartland, and by its fighting spirit, its broad shoulders, and its common sense.

Yet at the same time Chicago is also very much a world center—with its mighty industries exporting goods around the globe, and with its commodity markets linking international investors near and far.

Chicagoans and all Americans have every right to demand a foreign policy that serves their interests in concrete ways. They want a foreign policy that will build a safer world, a more prosperous world where their values can be secure.

That is exactly the kind of foreign policy that President Clinton has charged me to carry out. At the State Department, we

have a desk responsible for policy in virtually every foreign country: for example, there's a China desk, a Russian desk, and an
Egypt desk.

As Secretary of State, I'm determined that the State Department will have an "America desk" as well, and I will be sitting
behind it. My foremost mission is to advance the vital interests of
the citizens of the United States. Today, and over the coming
weeks and months, I want to outline how the Clinton administration plans to pursue that objective.

Our world has changed fundamentally in recent years. Walls
have come down. Empires have collapsed. Most important, the
Cold War is over. The Soviet Union is no more. Soviet Communism is dead. But so is the reference point that guided our policies
for 40 years. That reference point explained why our international leadership was so necessary; why our defense burden was
so heavy; and why our assistance to other countries was so critical.

Today, we face a world that is vastly more complex. It is a
world of breathtaking opportunities to expand democracy and
free markets. But it is also a world of grave new perils. Long-
simmering ethnic conflicts have flared. Weapons of mass destruction are falling into the hands of dangerous dictators. And new
global challenges cry out for attention, like the environment,
overpopulation, drug trafficking, and AIDS. Like the last generation's great leaders who met the challenge of the Cold War, we
need a new strategy for protecting and promoting American interests in the new era. We need a strategy that answers the questions that most Americans are now asking: Why, with the Soviet
threat gone, do we need to be active in the international scene?
Why must America still carry the burdens of leadership? Why,
when we urgently need renewal at home, should we continue to
dedicate resources abroad?

President Clinton has responded by laying out an American
foreign policy that is built on three pillars. *First,* building American prosperity. *Second,* modernizing of America's armed forces.
And *third,* promoting democracy abroad. The policy's fundamental premise is that in today's world, foreign and domestic policy
are inseparable. If we fail to maintain our strength at home, we
will be unable to lead abroad. Yet if we retreat into isolationism, it
will be impossible to revitalize our domestic strength. America
cannot thrive in a world of economic recession, violent conflicts,
and dictatorships.

It is no accident that President Clinton has identified promotion of America's economic security as the first pillar of our new foreign policy. We've entered an era where our economic competitiveness is vital to our ability to succeed abroad. As an essential first step, the President had put forth a bold program to get America's own economic house in order. It's a comprehensive strategy that will invest in the needs of our people, reduce our deficits, and lay the foundation for long-term economic growth.

The single most important step we can take to strengthen our position around the world is to enact the President's economic program, and to do it as soon as possible.

But steps at home cannot alone ensure America's prosperity. Today we are irreversibly linked to the global economy. Our lives are constantly touched by the huge flows of trade and finance that cross our borders. Over seven million Americans are now employed in export-related jobs.

Our ability to prosper in this global economy depends on our ability to compete. That means harnessing our diplomacy to serve our economic goals abroad: we must ensure that foreign markets are open to U.S. goods and U.S. investments. We must fight unfair competition against U.S. business and labor. And we must press the world's other financial powers to enact responsible policies that foster global growth.

The second pillar of our foreign policy will be modernizing our armed forces to meet new and continuing threats. The collapse of the Soviet Union enables us to significantly scale back our military establishment. Nonetheless, our power must always be sufficient to counter any threat to our vital interests. We must be able to deter and, when necessary, to defeat any potential foe. That's why we are taking steps to make our military more agile, mobile, flexible, and smart. We are determined to have the best equipped and the best trained fighting force in the world.

America cannot be the world's policeman. We cannot be responsible for settling every dispute or for answering every alarm. We are indispensable, but we cannot be indiscriminate.

Enlightened American leadership will require that we wisely marshal the West's collective strength. Ethnic conflicts, and the humanitarian disasters they generate, deeply offend our conscience. In many cases, they also pose a serious risk to international peace. And they produce thousands of refugees that can strain the political and economic stability of an entire region.

Our imperative is to develop the international means to contain and, more important, to *prevent* these conflicts before they

erupt. Here, it is critical that we use the United Nations in the
manner its founders intended. UN peacekeeping capabilities
must be strengthened to permit prompt, preventative action.
And our other instruments of collective security, such as the
NATO alliance, must be adapted to support the UN in these
efforts.

One of the most promising areas for preventive diplomacy is
in the Middle East. Here, the end of the Cold War has not un-
leashed conflict. Instead, it has created new chances for ending it.
I recently returned from the region, where I held extensive talks
with both Arabs and Israeli leaders.

I am convinced that there is a historic opportunity to take
strides toward peace in this troubled region. It is imperative that
all sides act to seize this opportunity and return to the negotiating
table in Washington on April 20th. If they do, the United States is
ready to act as a full partner in their efforts. If they do not, if they
allow this unique chance to slip away, another generation in the
Middle East could be lost to an endless cycle of confrontation and,
eventually, war.

Let me now turn to the third pillar of this Administration's
foreign policy: encouraging the global revolution for democracy
that is transforming our world. By helping promote democracy,
we do more than honor our deepest values. We are also making a
strategic investment in our nation's security. History has shown
that a world of more democracies is a safer world. It is a world
that will devote more to human development and less to human
destruction. And it is a world that will promote what all people
have in common rather than what tears them apart.

These three pillars—building American prosperity, modernizing America's armed forces, and promoting democratic
values—form the core of the Clinton administration's new American diplomacy. Now I would like to tell you how they converge
and also form the basis for one of our highest foreign priorities:
helping the Russian people build a free society and a market
economy. This is the greatest strategic challenge of our time.
Bringing Russia, one of our history's most powerful countries,
into the family of peaceful nations will serve our highest security,
moral, and economic interests.

For America and the world, the stakes are monumental. If we
succeed, we will have established the foundation for our lasting
security into the next century. But if Russia falls into anarchy or
lurches back to despotism, the price that we pay could be fright-

ening. Nothing less is involved than the possibility of a revived nuclear threat; higher U.S. defense budgets; spreading instability; and a devastating setback for the worldwide democratic movement. This deserves the attention of each and every American.

Over the days and weeks ahead, the Clinton administration will set forth a comprehensive strategy to support Russia's democracy and its efforts to build a market economy. My intention today is not to announce a detailed program of new initiatives. Rather, I would like to provide the strategic context for the approach we will follow. I want to explain the tremendous interest that we have in doing everything we can to help Russia's democracy succeed.

Let me stress that by focusing on Russia, I do not mean to neglect other new states. The well-being of the Ukraine, of Kazakhstan and Belarus, of Armenia, and of all the other former republics is a matter of utmost importance to America. We are fully committed to developing strong bilateral relations with each of these countries. We will support their independence and assist with their full integration into the world community. Indeed, it is partly out of concern for their welfare that I want to concentrate on Russia today. The fact is that the future security of Russia's neighbors depends heavily on the success of Russia's own democratic revolution.

Let us step back for a moment and look at the breathtaking benefits the end of the Cold War has brought to the United States and the world:

Historic agreements have been reached to slash the nuclear arsenals that threatened our country with annihilation.

The nations of the former Warsaw pact are free of Soviet domination and the burden of communism.

The possibility of a superpower conflict on the European continent has vanished, allowing us to bring thousands of troops home and to reduce the defense budget.

Around the globe, totalitarianism regimes that looked to the Soviet Union for support are isolated and on the defensive.

And from Vilnius to the Baltic to Vladivostok on the Pacific, vast new markets are slowly opening for Western business.

With a reforming Russia, all of these historic achievements were made possible. Without it, many may not be sustainable.

We stand again at a historic crossroads. It is reminiscent of the crossroads we faced in 1918 and 1945. Then, as now, we were summoned to lead the world in building a new peace. After World War I, we chose to retreat. And the consequences were disastrous.

After World War II, our leaders had the wisdom to answer the call. We fostered the institutions that re-built the free world's prosperity. And we helped lead a democratic alliance that contained and, ultimately, drained Soviet communism.

Today, for the third time this century, we have a historic opportunity to build a more secure world. We must redouble our efforts to help the Russian people as they struggle in an effort that has no historical precedent. With great courage, they are attempting to carry out these three simultaneous revolutions. First, transforming a totalitarian system into a democracy. Second, transforming a command economy into one based on free markets. And third, transforming an empire into a modern nation-state. If they succeed, we all will succeed.

Now it appears that another turning point has been reached in Russia's transition. For months, a constitutional crisis between President Yeltsin and the parliament has paralyzed Russian politics. That crisis has come to a head. President Yeltsin has called for a national plebiscite to resolve the constitutional impasse. In doing so, he has again demonstrated his faith in the only force that can guarantee reform's success: the Russian people.

We welcome President Yeltsin's assurance that civil liberties, including freedom of speech and the press, will be respected. We also welcome his firm rejection of imperial and Cold War policies. The most important point is that Russia must retain a democracy moving toward a market economy. That is the only basis for our new U.S.-Russian partnership.

The United States has strongly supported Russia's efforts to build democracy. Under President Yeltsin's leadership, historic progress has been made to establish a free society. We urge that this progress continue and that the Russian people be allowed to determine their future through peaceful means and with respect for civil liberties. On that basis, Russia can be assured of our full support in the difficult days ahead.

Today's crisis results in part from one indisputable fact: the pain of building a new system virtually from scratch is exacting a tremendous toll. The patience of the Russian people is wearing thin, a fact that is reflected in Russia's current political stalemate.

Nevertheless, over the last year, President Yeltsin and Russia's other democrats have demonstrated their commitment to reform. Civil liberties have been dramatically expanded. The military budget has been significantly cut. Prices have been freed in most sectors, and the result has been an end to the once ubiquitous lines that formed outside Russia's stores. Tens of thousands of shops, restaurants, and other small firms have been out in private hands. And a real start has been made on the difficult process of privatizing large enterprises. As a consequence, the share of the work force engaged in private commerce has more than doubled in the last two years.

Over the weekend, President Yeltsin re-committed his government to economic reform. He laid out in a clear and strong language the key elements of such a program: continued privatization of firms, selling land to farmers, stopping inflation, and stabilizing the ruble. If this program is implemented, our capacity to help will be greatly enhanced.

Russia's reformers are now looking to the West for support in this moment of extreme difficulty. The United States has a deep self-interest in responding to this historic challenge. We should extend to the Russian people not a hand of pity, but a hand of partnership. We must lead a long-term Western strategy of engagement for democracy.

In America, we cannot create a false choice between doing what is required to renew our economy at home, and doing what is necessary to protect our interests abroad. We must do both. During the long struggle of the Cold War, we kept the American Dream alive for all our people. At the same time, we made great sacrifices to protect our national security.

Today, we must meet that same challenge. To succeed, we must first change our mind sets. We need to understand that helping consolidate democracy in Russia is not a matter of charity, but a security concern of the highest order. It is no less important to our well-being than the need to contain a hostile Soviet Union was in an earlier day.

This week, in Washington, President Clinton and I will meet with Russia's foreign minister, Andrei Kozyrev. We will communicate our strong support for Russia's continued democratic development. And we will reiterate our concern that the current situation in Moscow must be resolved peacefully and in a way consistent with respect for civil liberties.

At this meeting with President Yeltsin next month in Vancouver, President Clinton intends to spell out the tangible steps we will take to assist Russian reform. The President is still considering the specific measures he will announce. But our bottom line is that we will be increasing and accelerating our support for Russian democracy. We cannot do it alone, but we must be prepared to do our part. Here, we favor a meeting later in April where the foreign and finance ministers of the leading industrial democracies will coordinate joint efforts to assist Russia's transformation.

As I said earlier, my task today is not to spell out specific initiatives. Nevertheless, I would like to offer a few thoughts on the issue of Western aid in general. Clearly, our assistance to Russia must be better targeted and better coordinated than it has been to date. It must focus on areas and constituencies in Russia that can have the greatest impact on reform's long-term success. It cannot simply be limited to public funds. Rather, it must catalyze our private sectors to take a leading role in Russia's transformation through trade, investment, and training. And our help must be felt at the grass roots level, to ease the pain of Russian children, workers, and senior citizens.

Despite its current economic difficulties, it is worth remembering that Russia is inherently a rich country. Its people are well educated. And its natural resource base exceeds that of any other country in the world. For example, Russia's oil reserves are huge and if properly exploited could probably finance much of Russia's economic reform. But today, thousands of aging oil wells and pipelines stand idle, decaying and in desperate need of critical spare parts. If Russia could find the means to repair them, the oil sold would be a lucrative source of foreign exchange that could be used to stabilize its economy.

One area where America's vital interests are directly engaged is the effort to dismantle the nuclear weapons of the Soviet Union. The $800 million program established by Senators Nunn and Lugar to destroy these weapons is a direct investment in our own security. Unfortunately, bottlenecks have allowed only a small fraction of this money to be used. Part of the delay has been caused by bureaucratic obstacles in Washington. We are committed to removing these obstacles. We want to see these weapons dismantled in the shortest possible time.

Another important goal we should have is strengthening the groups in Russia that will form the bulwark of a thriving democracy. Time after time, opinion polls of the Russian population show one thing: by large numbers, it is the younger generation that expresses the greatest support of democracy. They are the ones pushing for more economic freedom and for closer contacts with the West. Ultimately, whatever the result of today's political turmoil, this is the group that will carry the day for Russia's successful transition to democracy.

Through exchange programs, young Russians can be brought to the West and exposed to the workings of democracy and the market. Russian students, public officials, scientists, and businessmen are hungry for such experiences. Upon their return home, they can adapt their knowledge to best suit Russia's conditions. Perhaps most importantly, we can win long-term partners for freedom.

The existence of a strong, independent media is also essential for a democratic society. While Russia's free press has experienced tremendous growth in recent years, there is still a need for professional training of reporters, editors, and news managers. Here, Western technical assistance can make a difference.

Another area that deserves support is Russia's privatization effort. This process has continued across many of Russia's regions in spite of the recent political problems in Moscow. Putting private property into the hands of the Russian people is a critical step in building a free market economy. It will create millions of property owners and private entrepreneurs, a genuine middle class with a powerful stake in continued reform.

Of course, at the end of the day, Russia's progress toward the market and democracy cannot occur without an overhaul in the ground rules of the Russian economy. It will be vital to reduce the budget deficit, control the money supply, stabilize the ruble, and close down inefficient factories. But these are also the steps that will cause the greatest human pain and political risk. Again, Russia needs our help. The West must find a way to respond. And the response can't be limited to big promises with little delivery. We are now engaged in intensive consultations with our partners from the leading industrial democracies to develop a joint system of assistance.

Let me close by making two points. First, we must have no illusions. Even with our help, the road forward will be rocky. Setbacks are inevitable. Russia's transformation will take a great deal of hard work and probably a generation to complete.

As we meet, a great struggle is underway to determine the kind of nation Russia will be. However, as we focus on today's drama, it is important that we maintain a long-term perspective. Just as our vigilance in the Cold War took more than four decades to pay off, our commitment to Russia's democratic development must be for the duration. Our engagement with the reformers must be for the long haul: when they're out as well as when they're in, when they're down as well as when they're up.

However difficult things may be in the short run, we should have faith that the strategic course we have set—supporting democracy's triumph—is the correct one.

Second, we should know that any realistic program to assist Russian democracy won't be cheap. But there's no question that our nation can afford its fair share of an international effort. We can't afford to do otherwise. Together with the President, I am determined to work with Congress to find the funding. I am confident that the necessary resources can be found as we restructure our defense budget. But it will require bipartisanship. It will demand leadership and vision. And vitally, it will take a Russian partner that remains committed to democratic values and market reform.

At a time of great domestic challenge, some would say we should delay bold action in the foreign realm. But history will not wait. As Abraham Lincoln advised his countrymen, "We cannot escape history. We . . . will be remembered in spite of ourselves." Today, history is again calling our nation to decide anew whether we will lead or defer, whether we will shape this new era or instead be shaped by it. How will history remember us? I, for one, am confident that we will make the right choice: that we will be bold and brave in revitalizing our nation at home, while continuing to promote our interests and ideals abroad.

Thank you.

RENEWING THE DEMOCRATIC EXPERIENCE

DEMOCRACY IN AN AGE OF DENIAL[1]
TAYLOR BRANCH[2]

Every year, the Federation of State Humanities Councils invites members of Congress to a "Humanities on the Hill" breakfast to make them aware of the importance of the humanities in American life. The federation is an organization of humanities councils that exists in all of the states, the District of Columbia, Guam, Puerto Rico, and the Virgin Islands and which encourages public awareness and understanding of the humanities. It disseminates information on the humanities by sponsoring programs, exhibits, seminars, workshops and lectures.

The 1992 humanities breakfast was held at 9:00 A.M., on May 7, in room 106 of the Dirksen Senate Office Building in Washington D.C. It was attended by over 300 members of Congress, aides, state council staffs and board members.

The speaker at the breakfast was Taylor Branch, a journalist and author whose book, *Parting the Waters: America in the King Years, 1954–1963,* won the National Book Critics Circle award for non-fiction, the 1988 Christopher Award and the 1989 Pulitzer Prize in history. R. Z. Shepard, in *Time* magazine, describes the book as a "major accomplishment in biography as social history, voicing a widely held opinion."

Senator Harris Wofford, who inserted Branch's speech in the *Congressional Record,* remarked that Branch's *Parting the Waters . . .* "dramatically and perceptively described the great meeting of popular protest and public power that enabled us to achieve the two main goals of the civil rights movement—securing the right to vote for black Americans and striking down the walls of legal segregation." Senator Wofford further noted that "Mr. Branch's remarks before the State Humanities Councils remind each of us of what we have achieved, and of what we have yet to achieve." (August 6, 1992, S11812.)

[1]Delivered at the annual "Humanities on the Hill" breakfast, Dirksen Senate office building, Washington D.C., at 9:00 A.M. on May 7, 1992.

[2]For biographical note, see Appendix.

Taylor Branch, in this speech, entitled, "Democracy in an Age of Denial," discusses his experiences as a participant in the civil rights movement, what he has learned from studying the movement and what he believes must still be done to restore confidence in our democracy and our government.

Taylor Branch's speech: I'm happy to be with you this morning. You're good people assembled here in war council in bad times. My work is in history, and I call upon you partly as witnesses to a dilemma that I fear I will have when the second part of my history of the civil rights movement appears, whenever that is. I fear that few readers will believe that I began working on the book's opening scene three years before the Rodney King case. It is a 1962 police action in Los Angeles in which the LAPD raided a house of worship, beat and shot thirteen people, one of whom died, three of whom were shot in the testicles, all black men. Afterwards the victims were arrested and charged with riot, mayhem, and resisting arrest. All were criminally convicted. In effect it was what would have happened in the Rodney King case had there been no videotape. That happened in 1962. I treat the episode as a turning point in the life of Malcolm X and the life of black America. Yet one of the reasons that I spend so much time trying to recover the event is that it passed almost completely without notice in the world at large. That a trauma of that size could occur in a city like Los Angeles in 1962 without public notice is part of the history of this time. It's sobering in the sense that we see the recycling of this violence not just in 1965 in the Watts riot and again last week in the Rodney King riots, but also in 1962. It's hopeful in another sense, that in 1962 you could have even worse outrages and miscarriages of justice and not even have them noticed by the world at large. At least we've come some way from there.

The riot and the racial upheavals of the 1960s generally marked the beginning of the end of a democratic renewal that was the hopeful upsurge of the early civil rights movement. We here have to ask the difficult question, if the riots of 1992 follow the path of history and mark another inward turning in our time, where was the renewal that should have gone before? We've already started the withdrawal before we had the great expansion of hope. That is indeed a sobering thought.

Twenty-five years ago, I was a kid at Princeton, at graduate school, with a bare inclination that we had passed through a period of democratic renewal in the civil rights movement, which had forced a change in my life's interest against my will. My father is in the dry cleaning business, he brought me up to believe that all people who are interested in politics, and especially politicians, are those who cannot find honest work. The 1960s forced me to change that. In graduate school at the Woodrow Wilson School at Princeton, I wanted one chance to experience the civil rights movement before it faded away, and I persuaded my faculty review board, much against its will, to allow me to go down and work for John Lewis' voter education project in southwest Georgia. The faculty committee did not want me to go because they said non-institutional work was not policy relevant to experience; they wanted me to work for the Congressional Budget Office or preferably the Bureau of the Budget, which was and is considered the Taj Mahal of crisis management—that's what we called it back then. My proposal was considered an existential lark: I wanted to go down by myself, register these voters. The professors finally agreed that if I would agree to write a five-page memorandum on the policy implications of my existential experience for monopsony in the local labor markets of the agrarian counties of southwest Georgia. Back then, all freedom issues were considered a subsidiary of economic development. So I stepped off the end of the known world in going by myself into those rural counties. This is a personal story to tell you how my fascination with democratic history began only after I became a very disoriented young man.

In the summer of 1969, on the day men first landed on the moon, I was in a tiny little county, Schley County, in Georgia. After one month's work, I had given up on men. I decided that if there was any hope for voter registration in southwest Georgia, it was with the women. And in this tiny county I'd been told there was an old, old matriarch, 90 years old, and that if she could find it in her heart to say a kind word about voter registration in this county, where there were no black registered voters, that something might happen. So I was on her porch on July 20 [1969], the day Neil Armstrong had set foot on the moon. And I was trying to get her interested in voter registration, to receive a grant to register voters. She was in a rocking chair and had a lip full of snuff, and all of a sudden she said to me, "Young man, do you think we really landed on the moon this morning?"

And I said, "Yes," and she said, "How do you know?"

I said, "Well, I saw it on Walter Cronkite back at the motel before I came over here this morning."

She just rocked and she didn't say anything, and the next

thing she said was, "Have you seen the Simonize wax commercial?"

And I said, "What Simonize wax commercial?"

She said, "The one where the little children float across the
kitchen on an invisible shield of Simonize wax and don't scuff the
floor."

Actually, I remembered that, it was a very vivid commercial. I
said, "Yes, I've seen that."

She said, "Well, do you believe that?"

I realized she had an agenda going here, and I said, "Well,
yes, I believe that they can make it look like that, but that's a
commercial. I saw the moon landing on the news program. That's
different than a commercial."

She didn't say anything, she kept rocking. The next thing she
said was, "Have you ever been in a fist fight?"

Every time she threw me off balance I found myself talking
more and more in the language of policy. I said, "Unfortunately, I
have, I don't see it as a very good way of settling disputes," and so
on and so forth.

She said, "I mean the kind of fist fight when more than one
tooth gets knocked out at a time."

I said, "No, I've never been in one like that," and she said,
"Well, I've been in some, and I've seen plenty of them, and people
don't get up and talk again the way they do on 'Have Gun Will
Travel.'"

She kept rocking for awhile, and I kept talking more and
more about policy, getting more and more nervous, and finally
she said, "Young man, I can prove to you that we didn't land on
the moon this morning."

I said, "How can you do that?" She said, "Well, God wouldn't
allow it." Now being in the depth of a heathen period at that time,
I said, "What does God have to do with whether we landed on the
moon?"

She said, "You have not thought about it. If we could land on
the moon this morning, all we have to do is fill up our tank once
on the moon and on the next jump we could probably make it
into heaven without God's permission, without dying. And you
know that could never happen."

By that time, she really had me. I didn't know what to say, but
a number of lessons were dawning on me. One of them was that
she was not interested in voter registration in Schley County. I
perceived that. Another was that she was telling me in her own

way a very profound lesson about what is fear, what is real, who can teach what to whom. Here was a lady almost 90 years old who literally went back to the end of slavery, lived in a county with no black registered voters and where her whole life has taught her that questions of voting and race go to the very nerve of survival and identity and being. And all of a sudden, here on her porch one morning comes a young white man talking about economic development and voter registration, telling her, encouraging her to do something that she knows might mean life or death in that county. At her age she was not ready for it. She was asking me questions about what is real, what is hope, what is dangerous, what you can perceive, what is fear.

I also sensed something else: there was absolutely no way that I could capture the reality of that moment or that conversation, or a thousand other things that happened to me that summer, in the language of a policy memorandum for that faculty review committee back at Princeton. The language of policy does not reach the wisdom and experience of the common people in a democracy like ours. The old lady's presence made me feel this lesson in my bones long before I could articulate it, which is the point. I kept a diary that summer, as never before or since, just trying to record the experiences that I had traveling around. That became the basis of the first article I ever published, which occurred before it dawned on me that writing might be something for me to pursue as a career.

The old lady taught me a good deal about narrative, about democratic experience and where movements came from. "Movement" is a trivial word today. But a social movement is a fundamental faith in strangers and an encounter with new possibilities, always involving discovery and a step in the unknown. A fresh sense of democratic movements led to my strong, strong belief in narrative history, particularly in cross-cultural affairs. We make discoveries at the human level and not at the analytical level, although many people fool themselves into thinking that they can cross barriers between culture by analysis. It's an insight as old as the Book of Genesis that the truth of even the most complex abstractions is best communicated in stories about brothers quarreling with sisters or fathers quarreling with sons. We need narrative history. I think we especially need it in a democracy. We lose sight oftentimes of just how terrifying, how bold democracy really is. Democracy, in its best form, is a stark, public encounter with the inner nature of the human condition. It is by definition a faith in strangers, faith that the greatest issues of the day can turn on the vote of the last wino to come to the polls. We have more faith in strangers embedded in our tradition and in our fundamental philosophy than most of us care to contemplate. But this democracy, this vision, this movement, this opening of the public space, is basically what will save us and what will renew us if we hope to have another democratic renewal of the public faith in strangers to renew the democratic spirit in our time.

I like to think of what I've learned in studying movement history, civil rights history, cross-racial history, religious history in the last ten years, as a fundamental primer in democracy. The democratic faith in strangers requires a disciplined vision. It is a faith balanced by the discipline of self-control. We lose sight of the elementary fact that the heart of it is self-government, to govern ourselves without benefit of external authority. So a basic definition is that democracy is where the discipline of faith in strangers meets the disciplines of self-control. This is a sobering thought for these times, when we by and large have very little of either. In the generation since I met the lady rocking on her porch, white Americans have basically evacuated all large cities in the United States. We have turned inward. It is an era of white power, of suburban power, of Jewish power, black power, turning inward to tribal constituencies, rather than reaching out towards strangers. We have turned inward, we have very little faith in one another, and obviously, we have very little self-control. All we have to do is look at the budget, at schools and cities, at the environment, at some of the issues that make people concerned about the health of democracy today.

This is not the era for triumphalism, for crowing that democracy stands victorious at the end of history because the competing systems have fallen, particularly communism. There are other forms of government that are much older and better established, not only in history but in most parts of the world—than democracy, and those forms are tyranny, and chaos. Democracy will not survive unless people give it renewals of spirit. When Ben Franklin came out of the Constitutional Convention, he was asked, "What form of government have you conceived?" He said, "A new one, a democracy, if you can keep it." It was considered a bold and risky venture to conceive of a government without some external authority treating citizens like children and telling them what to do.

The under side of modern progress is that we have lost many

of the natural forms of discipline that once governed humankind. Famine, war, weather, crop failure, competition: many of these things checked our excesses through tragedy and hardship. We've triumphed over some of them, but we need to substitute a new source of discipline. The democratic belief is that it must come from within, sustained by our faith in one another and our belief in fundamental practices of citizenship. American history teaches that whenever the meaning of our democratic intuition is tested, when it is expanded, when leaders perform like geniuses and people perform like citizens, the focus has almost always been over the race issue. The race issue tells us how democratic we are becoming, in the age of the abolitionists as well as the age of Martin Luther King. Unfortunately, in the past generation, race has driven presidential politics in this inward turning period. The unspoken, prevailing message has been that government is evil because government exists to help poor people, which mainly means black people, and therefore we want to avoid it altogether. That subliminal message, in a sophisticated form, has driven our presidential politics to the degree that we have made government the enemy in a country dedicated to the notion that the government is us. How can we live with this kind of contradiction? It faces the Congress, it faces the humanities councils, so that we see democracy nowadays in these riots and in the budget questions, we see it drift, lost from its fundamental principles.

I see this to some degree in my own research in the secrecy issue. Some of the most ridiculous classifications and secrets going back to the 1930s and 1940s are still maintained today. The real Berlin Wall crumbled, which is a great miracle, but the paper Berlin Wall that separates our government from our people still stands proud. If you don't believe me, go to the F.B.I. reading room, which has no windows and where you can't go to the bathroom without an escort, and see some of the documents that still remain classified there, four, five decades later.

Another area where there is very little thinking about the fundamentals of democracy is the telltale realm of private vices. We are all over the place on the conflict between democracy's desire to protect people, to protect their freedoms, against its equivalent, competing goal of protecting people from harm by others. Cigarettes are terrible; they kill 350,000 people a year. We say that it should be against the law for children to smoke, but we sell cigarettes in vending machines. We say that drugs are a terrible thing, such that even a government premised on the notion

that people can govern themselves also operates on the premise
that those same people can't resist self-evidently self-destructive
devices without police to tell them what to do. Vices are monar-
chical in the response that they call out of people. At the same
time, we have state governments promoting lotteries, telling people that vice is not only something that they don't need to avoid,
but that it is their civic duty to participate. The ethos of the lottery
advertisement is very similar, almost identical, to the ethos of
your street corner drug dealer, which is "forget reality, forget
your obligation to the society, forget your children and take a
chance that you might hit and get high." Evocations in those ads
of what people should do and ought to do if they hit the lottery
are so antisocial that it mocks reality that they exist in a democracy. The fantasies portrayed have to do with buying castles or your
own personal moon rocket, escaping into material bliss, getting
away from the futility of work and the wretchedness of your
fellow creatures. Nothing that Donald Trump ever thought of
doing would embarrass the role models in lottery ads, who make
rubber barons look like models of civic virtue.

To recapture and renew the basics of democracy requires
clear thought, faith, discipline, and to some degree an enlarge-
ment of the public space. As the world shrinks we have to face the
fact that we Americans are rich, we have to speak plain, like the
lady in the rocking chair, we have to understand that we can't all
be middle class, that by world standards anybody who makes
$10,000 or $15,000 is rich. We have a country that is paralyzed
because we have a large number of people who are too puffed
up to realize that the great challenge in the modern world is
what sacrifices we are willing to make for our future, for our
progeny, for our public space. Marginal private consumption of
people even at the middle-class level is not as important as whether we pass on the democratic experiment alive and well in spirit.
To do so requires enormous discipline and connection with
strangers.

In the period I'm writing about now, one of the most moving
displays of such disciplined faith occurred in the final moments of
Mickey Schwerner. I've spoken with several of the FBI agents
who took the confessions of the Klansmen who killed Schwerner
and two other civil rights workers in June '64. The agents were
struck by something: that all the Klansmen remembered the same
haunting words from their victim. When he was dragged out into
the Mississippi night, knowing that he was about to be lynched,

facing people full of hate, Schwerner's last words before he was shot were "Sir, I know just how you feel." The discipline of the movement was that even when confronting death itself and your worst enemies, you never broke hope of establishing human contact with your fellow citizens. Such incandescent faith cannot last long. Within two years of that remark by Schwerner, which was fully in keeping with the preaching and the discipline of the freedom riders, people who had built a movement by reaching out for common ground with their enemies were instead chopping off ground even among their own allies, saying "you're not militant enough for me," or "you're only a liberal, I'm a radical," and they started turning inward. People can't afford to do that. It is rejecting the discipline and the hope of the democratic spirit.

Looking back after ten years' research, I have a number of odd thoughts on the historical challenge of renewing the democratic experience. I'll mention just two. Number one, the last time the United States had a balanced budget was in 1968, the year of the Tet offensive, the Martin Luther King riots, the Robert Kennedy assassination, the King assassination, the peak year of the Vietnam war, and the only major year of the war on poverty. The President who introduced that budget and who got it through was Lyndon Johnson, the father of the Great Society. If we have accepted the political paradox that only a bedrock conservative can have the potential capital to open the door to communist China, perhaps we need to begin to entertain the notion that only a social liberal who aches for the poor can have the discipline to regain our sense of budgetary discipline in our country. How many trillions of debt must we heap on our children before that possibility occurs?

The second odd thought has to do with women, like the old woman in the rocking chair. If the periods of renewal, of movement spirit, of expansion in the public consciousness occur most often in American history around the race issue, it also seems true that those movements have been built upon the sensibilities of women in alliance with the maverick clergy. When you're looking for people to go to jail, when you're looking for plaintiffs, they are more likely to be women. And when you need a public spokesman, that spokesman is going to speak the language of Isaiah, the language of Amos and of the other justice prophets of Hebrew scripture. That's true of the age of Theodore Parker, and true in the age of Martin Luther King, who quoted Parker: "The arc of the moral universe is long, but it bends towards justice." That message, and the purity of the notion that democratic intuition is married to something that's very close to the heart of both our religious impulses and of our highest civic duty, seems to come through the sensibilities and the manpower, if you will, of women. From this perspective, it is a tragedy that the abortion issue in the last 25 years has to some degree divided women from the clergy. We need either more women clergy or more of the prophetic clergy in consultation with women, to restore a coalition that has wrestled illumination and hope for eras far more gloomy than our own.

Finally, for your humanities councils and in the spirit of democratic renewal, I would like to recommend something that I have grown with in conviction ever since I met the woman in the rocking chair, which is the value of oral history. My interview with her was of oral history. I would not have found her lessons in a library. Cultures tend to preserve what they are comfortable with. Fifty years from now, if someone wants to write about the impact of Asian-American immigration in the United States in the '80s and '90s, they probably will not find the documents to bring it alive in libraries. Oral history is important not just for the raw materials of living history but as an antidote to television and other forces in our modern age that shear us from one another, generation from generation, grandparents from grandchildren, black from white, Asian from European, all these divides that are so crucial and so paralytic to democratic change and to understanding our history. I believe that oral history is a rectifying force not just in overcoming the great tragedy of vanished, unrecoverable history. If you go to Alabama today and ask for the oral histories of the bus boycott in Montgomery or the Selma march, they will look at you like you're nuts, but as teaching tool for the people, like myself, who go and do those oral histories. In your state humanities councils, I encourage you to explore the notion of having teenagers and little school children in American history courses do oral histories with their own grandparents or other relatives, to rekindle, to rediscover the human sinews of family, these differences within the generation. They may move on to do an oral history of a grandparent of somebody else's family, particularly from a different culture. Then you've got the beginnings of what a movement is—a discovery that the world is larger than its material boundaries, and that they themselves can make it larger. That sense of stepping into the unknown is the beginning of faith in strangers, and I hope that it will renew the democratic spirit as has constantly occurred when people really apply themselves to that central intuition of our American history.

If democracy is all that's left, we must try it. And never, never take it for granted.

SHALL WE OVERCOME?[1]
F. FORRESTER CHURCH[2]

On January 18, 1993, for the first time since Congress established it as a federal holiday, Martin Luther King Day was celebrated in all fifty states. Across the country, ceremonies were held honoring Dr. King, who, if he had not been slain 25 years ago, on April 4, 1968, would have been 64 years old on January 15, 1993.

Participants in the ceremonies included the mighty and the unknown. At Howard University, in Washington D.C., President-elect Bill Clinton addressed more than 1,000 local officials and their friends. In Atlanta, Coretta Scott King, widow of the civil rights leader, called for a moratorium on violence. The Reverend Jesse Jackson, who was with King when he was killed; the Reverend Bernice King, King's youngest daughter; Jean Bertrand Aristide, the ousted president of Haiti; Eleanor Holmes Norton as well as several prominent civil rights leaders and government officials all took part in various observances of Martin Luther King Day which occurred throughout the country. In Los Angeles, more than a thousand people marched to celebrate the first King Day since the riots of the previous summer.

Among the many memorable addresses given in observance of Martin Luther King Day, a particularly interesting and unusual sermon was delivered by a white clergyman to an affluent, predominantly white congregation on New York City's upper east side. The speaker was the Reverend F. Forrester Church, pastor of the Unitarian Church of All Souls on Lexington Avenue and 80th Street. His audience, were typical churchgoers attending the regular Sunday morning services. Reverend Church entitled his sermon—"Shall We Overcome?".

[1]Delivered at the 10:00 A.M. and 11:15 A.M. services, at the Unitarian Church of All Souls, New York City, on January 17, 1993.

[2]For biographical note, see Appendix.

In the course of his remarks, Church discussed his difficulty in preparing the sermon:

> It should be an easy sermon, but it's not. The reason it's not, is that I am more aware than ever that my own life experience is so radically different than that of any person of color in this country—that for me to wax eloquent on the evils of racism would be a benign but basically hollow exercise. I know little, first hand, about the evils of racism.

Church also discusses the shortcomings of his own background, his experience in trying to understand the problems of minorities, and the difficulty of trying to put himself in their shoes.

Dr. Church delivered the sermon at two services on Sunday, January 17, 1993: at 10 A.M. before an audience of 150; and at 11:15 A.M. to about 450 congregants. Preceding the sermons were a prelude, a tenor solo, the doxology, a hymn, a prayer and a rendition of Dr. King's favorite anthem, "Precious Lord." After the sermon came a hymn, "America the Beautiful," the benediction, and a postlude. The 10 o'clock service included a talk in which a member of the church shared her memories of Dr. King, whom she had known as a child.

Reverend Church's sermon: Holidays exist for two reasons. The first might be called the "gathering" or "significant cause." We take time off to ponder something essential or meaningful in the lives we share. All religious and national holidays spring from some deep collective need to ponder or celebrate, to mourn or give thanks. They exist as compass points for our souls.

But they exist for another reason as well. Even those who participate in the religious or patriotic ceremonies that mark these holidays tend to lapse into a primary appreciation of their secondary cause, vacation. The long weekend, the gift of a little discretionary time, closed schools, the luxury of an extra day off. We need that too. We need occasions that break the tyranny of a daily grind. We need to vacate, to relax. In and of itself that is a good thing.

But because it is a good thing, we can easily overlook the reason we have been given this time. We can overlook what it was that caused our forebears to establish a holiday in the first place. Veteran's Day, Columbus Day, President's Day, all have become basically interchangeable national holidays almost completely stripped of their essential or original meaning. They are plain vanilla, white bread, all-American three-day weekends. We look forward to them not in anticipation of honoring those who have served our country in war, died for our country, participated in the union movement, or whatever. We look forward to them because we get a Monday off.

Not all of us get tomorrow off. That is probably not a bad thing, because, so far anyway, the newest of our national holidays is, for many of us, still more a day on than a day off. It hasn't been homogenized or pasteurized into a generic celebration. And, for better or worse, it won't be for some time, because what it celebrates has yet to come to pass.

More than any other, Martin Luther King day is the quintessential American patriotic holiday. Through the pain of its true sponsors, it harkens back to the aspirations of our founders and passions of our prophets. It permits us no easy celebrations, no mindless, instantly forgotten rituals, because, the moment we pay attention, it reminds us that we have yet to overcome our own prejudices and fears. If we are paying any attention at all, it reminds us of just how far we have to go to break down the many barriers between people that subvert the idealistic blueprint for this republic, *E Pluribus Unum,* out of many, one.

I had a harder time than usual writing this morning's sermon. In fact, I threw away my first two drafts. Martin Luther King Sunday should cause no difficulty for any liberal minister. King was influenced by several liberal ministers, past and present, especially during his student days in Boston. And his theology— thick in ethics, thin in metaphysics—fits easily into this pulpit. I could tell stories about how members of this very congregation witnessed along Martin Luther King's side during the most difficult and important days of the civil rights struggle in the mid- sixties. I could even talk about my father, who, as a 33 year-old U.S. Senator, was asked by Lyndon Johnson to serve as the assistant floor manager for the 1957 Civil Rights Act, and who, despite the fact that only 500 blacks lived in Idaho, never cast a vote against a major piece of civil rights legislation during his 24 years in the Senate.

It should be an easy sermon, but it's not. The reason it's not is that I am more aware than ever that my own life experience is so radically different than that of any person of color in this country that for me to wax eloquent on the evils of racism would be a benign but basically hollow exercise. I know little, first hand, about the evils of racism. Three hours in a movie theater watching Spike Lee's *Malcolm X* proved that point. I could and did sympathize profoundly, but to empathize, to get in someone else's skin and feel what they feel, is a different matter entirely. The most

important thing I learned while watching that movie is how enormous the gap is between my own experience of growing up and
that of almost every black African-American or any other ethnic
or religious minority in our society.

Let me tell you a little about the two sermons I wrote this week
that you are not going to hear this morning. The first you would
have liked. It was about the importance of continuing our efforts
to cross 96th Street, to work with our sister congregation and our
adopted school, to enhance our work with the Children's Task
Force, the AIDS Task Force, our soup kitchens and scout troops,
to build up our service programs not only by offering more help
to our neighbors. All of this fulfills Martin Luther King Jr.'s Social
Gospel. It was an unobjectionable, very boring sermon, and I
canned it.

The second sermon you would not have liked. It pointed out
that we were a basically rich Upper East Side congregation of
unselfconscious racists who think far more highly than we ought
to of ourselves.

The third sermon, which, awkward though it may be, you are
now hearing, is poised somewhere uncomfortably between the
first two. We are doing good things in this church. But for us—
not others but us—to benefit fully from these things, we must
examine ourselves and our own inheritance of privilege a little
more closely.

Robert Coles has written several books about children, rich
and poor, black and white. One of the books he wrote was about
me and most of us. As a child of social privilege—not wealth but
privilege—I grew up with what Coles calls a "sense of entitlement." I assumed that I could do anything, be anything. In contrast, for so many others in our society entitlement and privilege
can only be won at tremendous cost, and even when won, remains
precarious.

Think about it this way. What would it be like to be unwanted?
An unwanted child, an unwanted neighbor, an unwanted race.
Not unneeded, unwanted. A problem for society. A burden. A
price tag. Your fate to be carved on the public plate, every social
program a piece of meat offered by do-good liberals and pulled
away by financially responsible conservatives. And then, when the
pain became too great, when you spoke out or acted out, you are
branded as ungrateful or counter-productive. How do you get it
right? How do you contribute and excel if you start out life as a
problem?

My great-grandmother, who grew up in Idaho with Indians as neighbors, was fond of saying that you cannot know another's pain unless you walk a mile in his or her moccasins. How does a child of entitlement fit his or her feet into the shoes of a child of unentitlement? What we usually do is to tell them to work hard in school, avoid drugs, do all the things that we ourselves did successfully, at least part of the time, without ever having to think about ourselves as problem cases. Yet, for someone who has wants and needs just like us, but is born unwanted, it's completely different. Until we can begin to understand how different it is, we just won't get it.

I don't care how liberal you are. The problem is that we children of entitlement, (and nine out of ten of us here this morning fit the bill), can help to ease the pain of the unentitled far more easily than we can feel their pain. As long as this remains the case, those we help are as likely to turn their backs on us as they are to thank us. And then we, feeling hurt, may well turn on them. Resist the temptation. There is nothing noble about people of privilege feeling sorry for themselves for being misunderstood.

So how shall we break the lock? I have only one idea, and I am not sure how often it will work. Step back and recall how you act and feel when you are, or sense you are, unwanted. It happens to each of us, probably every day. We enter a room and it feels like the wrong room; everyone else seems at home; we don't know what to do, or even how to get out without some painful encounter. Or we have been rejected or ignored by someone whose help we need or opinion we value. Every child of privilege is also at times an unwanted child. We know that and we feel it. We just don't like to think of ourselves that way.

By the same token, every unwanted child can earn, through far harder work than most of us could easily imagine, a sense of entitlement. That is one thing about this country. It can be done. But for it to happen in anything like an evenhanded way, more than a few pairs of moccasins will have to be exchanged. Somehow, the unwanted child in each of us will have to find a way to reach out to other, unwanted children, make a real connection, and find that this connection constitutes the greatest privilege of all, communion, friendship, compassion, even love.

Capturing the difficulty we face in celebrating this holiday, perhaps the most important speech delivered this week was by a 17-year-old black student at Horace Mann School.

"Dr. King's dream has not come true for me," said student

body president Sheldon Golber, according to a report in the *Daily News*. "There is no symphony of brotherhood in America. Everything is messed up."

His eyes glistened as he recalled a visit to Italy, when he was the first black person to visit a rural mountain village and the people accepted him. He took a little black rock home with him, calling it a stone of hope.

"Now what do I do with it?" he asked. "Do I use it like my Palestinian brothers in the West Bank, or my African brothers in the streets of Johannesburg? Or will it be used against me as I am chased from the streets of Bensonhurst?"

Again we are reminded, there is no easy way out, no easy way to build the bridge to Martin Luther King Jr.'s dream. Yet, his dream is simple. It is predicated on the fact that we are all human, flawed and filled with promise. Whether children of entitlement or unentitlement, we are all children of God.

How do we realize this? Perhaps if we can draw from our own limited experience of being problem children, unwanted, in the way, out of place, perhaps if we can store it in our memory and bring it out when children who are really without privilege struggle in our midst for some respect or hope or love, we will see our own tears in their eyes.

How much better this, how much more helpful than drawing from our strengths—not the weaknesses we share but the strengths that come more easily—to offer our support.

The support we offer is good, not bad. I know that. But it fails to provide the one thing most needful, for us and for those we seek to help: recognizing that we are truly one, one people who know how to suffer, and can identify with others to help them emerge from their own pain.

This may sound a little sentimental, a little pious: to draw from our weakness to tap another's strength. Perhaps it is. But it is also Biblical. To empty ourselves and be filled. To lose ourselves and be found. It is Gospel. Good news.

One more piece of good news. This is a new holiday we are celebrating. We still have a little time to begin to get it right.

COLUMBUS PLUS 500 YEARS:[1]
WHITHER THE AMERICAN INDIAN?
David Archambault[2]

The 1992 quincentennial celebration of Christopher Columbus's voyage to the New World evoked not only praise and celebration, but also condemnation and controversy. Five hundred years after the event, historians and biographers debate whether the remarkable journey was a blessing or a curse for the world.

Native Americans have long held mixed feelings for Columbus's voyage, as their lives, and the lives of their ancestors, were radically affected by his four trips to the New World. David Archambault, a member of the Hunkpapa band of the Lakota tribe, and a member of the Sioux nation, addresses this issue frequently as he spoke to groups across the United States during 1992–1993. As President of the American Indian College Fund, Archambault aims to accomplish two things in his speeches: to let America know about his people, their past, and what they are now doing for themselves, and to inform the public about the Fund.

Modeled on the United Negro College Fund, the American Indian College Fund is a non-profit organization that seeks to win financial support from the public at large. Founded by tribal presidents, the Fund was organized to address two problems: first, for the most part, state support for tribal colleges is not available because many tribes have a sovereign-nation relationship with the federal government, and second, young Indians who leave the reservation to attend college have an extremely high dropout rate. Statistics show that about 90% of American Indians, attending non-Indian colleges, leave without graduating, while 35% of those studying at tribal colleges graduate, with another 53% finding jobs after leaving.

One reporter described Archambault, a 45-year-old man, who wears dapper business suits and a long ponytail, as an eloquent spokesman for the American Indian College Fund. (Mike Allen, *San Diego Transcript,* April 9, 1993, p. 1)

Archambault, who holds a bachelor's degree in education

[1]Delivered to the Rotary Club of Murray, Utah, on April 6, 1992.
[2]For biographical note, see Appendix.

from Black Hills State College and a master's degree in educational administration from Pennsylvania State University, taught at two other tribal colleges before he became president of Standing Rock College.

On a two year leave of absence from Standing Rock College, Archambault delivered the following speech on April 6, 1992 to an audience of about 150 people at the weekly meeting of the Murray, Utah, Rotary Club.

David Archambault's speech: Thank you and good afternoon. *Hau Kola.* That is how we Lakota say "Greeting, Friends." I am happy to be here today to represent Native American people. I am a *Ikoeya Wicaska,* an ordinary man. We think of an ordinary man as not superior to anyone else or for that matter to anything else. We, all people and all things, are related to each other.

We begin our spiritual ceremonies with the phrase *Onitakuya Oyasi,* which means all my relations. We believe that all people are ultimately part of one nation, the nation of mankind, but that this nation is only one of many nations that inhibit the mother earth. To us all living things are nations: the deer, the horses, things that crawl, things that fly, things that grow in and on the ground. All of these nations were created by the same power, and none is superior to another. All are necessary for life. We are expected to live and work in harmony.

In my travels I have learned that many Americans in mainstream society are uninformed or ill-informed about American Indians.

So let me begin by responding to questions people most often ask about us, or questions people might most like to ask.

No, we don't consider that Christopher Columbus discovered America. Estimates of the number of people who lived in the so-called New World at the time Columbus arrived run from 40 to 100 million or more. Hey, we knew we were here. It was Columbus who was lost. Maybe that poem ought to say, "When Columbus sailed the ocean blue, it was he, not America, who got discovered in fourteen hundred ninety-two."

Yes, American Indians are American citizens. After World War I, a nation grateful for the contributions of Indians to the war effort made all American Indians full citizens.

No, we are not prisoners on the reservations. We can leave any time. Many have. But the rest of us don't want to. We don't want to be assimilated into the dominant culture. We want to preserve our own culture and traditions. I'll tell you later how I hope to do that.

Yes, we have a unique status in the United States. We are both citizens and sovereign people. That comes from our history as nations, or tribes, defeated by Europeans, who, after giving up on trying to Christianize and civilize us, recognized our right to self-determination. I'll come back to this, too.

No, not all Indians are alike. There is diversity among tribal nations just as there is among European nations. American Indians in 500 or so tribes speak more than 200 languages and dialects.

Yes, many Americans have an especially tough time of it today with alcohol and other health problems, with poverty and inadequate education and job opportunities, and with just trying to figure out their own identity. Only we Indians can provide the leadership needed to solve these problems.

Finally, no, we don't care, at least most of us don't, whether you call us Indians, Native Americans, Indigenous People, or Amerinds. An Indian comedian tells it this way: "I know why white people call us Indians," he says. "When Columbus got here, he thought he had arrived in the Indies, so naturally he called the inhabitants Indians. I'm just thankful he didn't think he arrived in Turkey."

Today I want to share with you some of our history and culture and hopes for the future. It is important to American Indians, and I think to you as well, that **all** Americans know more about the first people to come to this land, about where we are and what we are doing and where we are headed. If we are to respect our differences and value what we have in common, we just begin with understanding.

During this quincentenary of Columbus' voyage, attention is once again focused on what the white man brought to this land and on Columbus himself. The man who made such a remarkable journey has become the stuff of legend as well as history. He is admired and detested, exalted and condemned. Columbus day will surely never be a favorite holiday among Indians, but we should consider Columbus for what he was, not for what we may wish he had been.

Columbus was a skilled and courageous mariner who led his ships across unchartered waters. He found land and people unknown to Europeans. He discovered a sea route between Europe and America. Never mind that Norse explorers and perhaps others had made the trip earlier. It was Columbus who recorded ways for others to make it across the waters, and back again.

Columbus came here, however, not to trade, but to conquer; he came here to enrich himself and enslave his captives. His mission, in the words of his royal charter, was to "discover and acquire" all new lands as well as "pearls, precious stones, gold, silver," and other valuables. He would write back to Spain, "From here, in the name of the Blessed Trinity, we can send all of the slaves that can be sold."

Columbus was a man of his time. He felt inspired by his god, empowered by his monarch, and reassured by the rightness of his cause. He was sailing, as the saying had it, for "God, glory, and gold." If he objected to enslaving others and taking their lands, someone else may have gotten that royal charter. To me, Columbus is neither hero nor villain, but rather a symbol of a world forevermore transformed. His culture and mine have never fully made peace.

Tens of millions of native people would die during and after the years of Columbus's four voyages to our shores: die of gunfire from soldiers who wanted their lands and precious metals; die of maltreatment while forced to work as slaves; die of white man's diseases, such as smallpox and typhoid, for which they had no immunity.

These native people had been hunters and fishermen and gatherers and farmers and weavers and traders. They had created stable, even advanced societies. They had highly developed agricultural and trading systems. It was they who had grown the first potatoes and had the first corn and the first tomatoes. They understood mathematics and architecture and calendar systems. They were rich in art and culture as well as in gold and silver. The Incas, the Mayans, the Aztecs, and many others, civilizations all destroyed, their people subjugated.

In North America, too, Indians lost their lands, their economy, and their freedom to Europeans. At times, the new settlers were not quite sure what to do about these native people. The Indians had welcomed them, fed them, traded with them. They were people who respected their environment. They had developed intricate political and social systems. The Iroquois, for example, had the world's oldest true democracy: a Supreme Chief, a legislative council, and a judicial branch as well as universal suffrage and direct representation. It was a system the Founding Fathers of the new nation would study and learn from.

But the Indians were in the way, in the way of new settlements and new riches. So for a long time, the objective was to get rid of the Indian. "The only good Indian is a dead Indian," the saying went. Whites even slaughtered the buffalos so the Indian could not hunt. The Indians fought back, often ferociously, but they lacked the manpower and the arms to resist.

Sometimes they pleaded. In a remarkable speech in 1879, Chief Joseph of the Nez Indians addressed his conquerors with these words: "All men were made by the same great Spirit Chief," he said. "They are all brothers and all should have equal rights. . . . Let me be a free man, free to talk and think and act for myself, and I will obey all of your laws."

Often they made treaties: 800 of them, in fact, nearly half of which were ratified by the U.S. Senate in full accord with the federal Constitution. Each of these treaties—every one—was violated by a nation that prides itself on keeping its word.

The Indians could not resist, but they could not be exterminated either. And so the government moved them to reservations, a movement with a long and sordid history. One of the most notorious chapters in that history was recorded in the 1830s when tens of thousands of Cherokees, Choctaws, and Creeks were forcibly moved from the southeastern United States to what is now the state of Oklahoma. The Cherokees called it the "trail of tears." Along the way, nearly one-quarter of them died of starvation and disease.

The reservations were run by those who believed the way to "civilize" us was to take away our language and culture and religion. Our children were called savages and taken from us. They were put in boarding schools where they were educated—dare we say "brainwashed"?—with the white man's ways. Their teachers vowed to "kill the Indian and save the child." The idea was that if the white man couldn't get rid of the Indian, perhaps he could at least get rid of the Indian's culture.

Not until the 1930s was an effort made to give Indians limited sovereignty, allowing them to carry on their traditions and pass along their culture to their children.

By the 1950s, the new watchword was assimilation: break up the tribes, move Indians into mainstream society. In other words, make them "real Americans." Once again the emphasis was on destroying Indian culture.

Only during the past several decades has there been a growing realization that we American Indians must determine our own destiny. We must be free to cherish our traditions and our culture, but also learn to live and work with society around us. We must learn to walk in both worlds.

Can we do it? Yes, we can. It will require education and economic development and self-sufficiency. It demands that we create opportunity and hope for future generations.

This idea is not original with me. It was taught to us by a great leader of the Lakota people, my people, the great chief Sitting Bull. He taught us that Indian children could succeed in modern society and yet retain the values of their culture, values such as respect for the earth, for wildlife, for rivers and streams, for plants and trees; and values such as caring for each other and for family and community.

He taught us that we must leave behind more hope than we found. "Let us put our minds together," he said, "and see what life we can make for the children."

That is why there is an American Indian College Fund. It is to carry out the dream of Sitting Bull: to bring together the best mind in the Indian and non-Indian world to build a better future for our children. Our mission is twofold: to raise the badly needed funds, of course, but also to help the general public understand the heritage of American Indians.

There are 26 colleges located on or near reservations in the United States. They were created by and for Indians. Three are four-year colleges; the others, two-year schools. Most are fully accredited and the rest are earning accreditation.

In these schools, our children are prepared for both worlds. The schools maintain a rigorous academic discipline while preserving Indian heritage and culture. Our students study math and science and business management as well as American Indian philosophy, traditions, and language. They learn what it means to be Indian, and gain a greater understanding of the world around them.

And it's working. Young American Indians who attend our colleges go on to further education and employment. They become productive, active citizens with confidence and pride to their tribal heritage. Many return to the reservation to work. Above all, they learn to value learning, and to value the wisdom of those who came before us.

The colleges do something more. They serve their communities. They offer job training and day care, health clinics and counseling services, public-affairs and literacy programs. They provide leadership and support for economic development of the reservations. In short, they are committed to service and renewal.

Not long ago researchers from the Carnegie Foundation for

the Advancement of Teaching spent two years studying our colleges. The schools, the Foundation concluded, "are crucial to the future of Native Americans and to the future of our nation." The foundation called accomplishments of the schools "enormously impressive" and said they "give hope to students and a new life to their communities."

But the report also pointed to the need for expanded science labs and libraries and urged the federal government to keep the promise it has made. Congress had authorized payment of nearly $6,000 for each full-time equivalent student at tribal colleges. But the amount actually appropriated is only about half that.

I feel a special commitment to the work of these colleges, not only because I temporarily head the effort to raise private funds and public awareness for them but, more important, because of what they mean to my life and the lives of my people.

More than 100 years ago, our great chief Sitting Bull was murdered. His people, frightened that they too would be killed, set out on foot across South Dakota along with Chief Big Foot. Carrying their children, they fled across the frozen prairie through the bitter subzero cold 200 miles to seek refuge on the Pine Ridge reservation in southwestern South Dakota.

On December 29, 1890, near a creek now known to all the world as Wounded Knee, Chief Big Foot and his followers were massacred. No one knows who fired first, but when the shooting was over, nearly 300 Indians—men, women, and children—lay dead and dying across the valley. Their bodies were dumped into a mass grave. The survivors were unable to hold a burial ceremony, a ceremony we call the wiping away of tears. It meant the living could never be free.

On the 100th anniversary of the Massacre at Wounded Knee, several hundred of us on horseback retraced the journey of Big Foot and his band during those final days. We arrived at dawn at the site of the mass grave at Wounded Knee and completed the wiping of the tears ceremony. The Si Tanka Wokiksuye, the Chief Big Foot Memorial Ride, was a mourning ritual that released the spirits of our ancestors and closed a tragic chapter in our history.

We have the opportunity now to help rebuild our nation. And I do not mean just the Indian nations. On this 500th anniversary of Columbus's voyages, we together can build a better America, a nation enriched by the diversity of its people and strengthened by the values that bring us together as a community.

Let us make this anniversary a time of healing and a time of renewal, a time to wipe away the tears. Let us, both Indian and non-Indian, put our minds together and see what life we can make for our children. Let us leave behind more hope than we found. I think Sitting Bull would be proud of us all.

Thank you. *Tosha Akin Wanchin.*

A THOUSAND THOMAS JEFFERSONS[1]
Carl Sagan[2]

The date, the place, and the speaker were ideal for the naturalization ceremonies which granted United States citizenship to a group of people from 31 different countries.

The date was July 4, 1992—Independence Day.

The site was the east portico—the back of the nickel—of Thomas Jefferson's home in Monticello, Virginia.

The speaker was Dr. Carl Sagan, professor of astronomy and space science, director of the Laboratory for Planetary Studies at Cornell University. Dr. Sagan is also a Pulitzer Prize winning author, the narrator of the highly acclaimed television series *Cosmos* and an effective and popular speaker who does not restrict his public speaking to scientific topics.

In this address, Sagan identifies his own interests and concerns as a scientist and as a firm believer in democracy. He identifies his values with those of Thomas Jefferson and he challenges the newly naturalized citizens to exercise their rights and mold their lives in an effort to become the Thomas Jeffersons of today.

Carl Sagan's speech: Thomas Jefferson was a scientist. Or, at least, that's how he described himself. If you visit his home here at Monticello, if you enter those doors, you can find abundant evidence of his scientific interests, not just in his immense and varied library, but in copying machines, automatic doors, telescopes, and

---

[1] Delivered on the occasion of naturalization of citizens of 31 foreign nations, from the east portico of Thomas Jefferson's home at Monticello, Virginia, on July 4, 1992.

[2] For biographical note, see Appendix.

other instruments, some at the cutting edge of early nineteenth-century technology. Nature destined him, he said, to be a scientist, but there were no opportunities for scientists in pre-revolutionary Virginia. Other, more urgent, needs took precedence. He threw himself into the historic events that were transpiring around him. Once independence was won, he said, later generations could devote themselves to science and scholarship.

Jefferson was a childhood hero of mine, not because of his scientific interests, but because he, almost more than anyone else, was responsible for the spread of democracy throughout the world. The idea—breathtaking, radical, and revolutionary at the time (in some places in the world, it still is)—is that not kings, not priests, not big city bosses, not dictators, but ordinary people, working together, are to rule the nation. Not only was Jefferson a leading theoretician of this cause; he was involved in the most practical way, helping to bring about the great American political experiment that has, all over the world, been emulated or longed for since then.

Jefferson died here on July 4th, 1826, exactly fifty years after the colonies issued a stirring document, written by Jefferson, called the Declaration of Independence. It was denounced by conservatives worldwide. In his eyes, these two interests, science and democracy, were connected. In a letter composed a few days before that fiftieth anniversary, a few days before his death, he wrote that it was the light of science that had demonstrated that "the mass of mankind has not been born with saddles on their backs," nor were a favored few born "booted and spurred." He wrote in the Declaration of Independence that we all must have the same opportunities, the same inalienable rights. And if the definition of "all" was painfully restrictive at the time, the spirit of the Declaration was generous enough that today "all" really does mean every one of us.

Jefferson was a student of history, not just the compliant and safe history that praises our own time or country or ethnic group, but the real history of real humans, our weaknesses as well as our strengths. History taught him that the rich and powerful will steal and oppress if given half a chance, that power corrupts. He described the governments of Europe, which he saw at first hand as the American ambassador to France. Under the pretense of government, he said, they have divided their nations into two classes: wolves and sheep. Jefferson taught that every government degenerates when it is left to the rulers alone, because rulers, by the very act of ruling, misuse the public trust. The people themselves, he said, are the only safe repository of power.

But the people, he argued, are easily misled. And so he advocated some safeguards, some insurance policies. One was the constitutional separation of powers so that various groups, pursuing their own selfish interests, balance one another, preventing any one of them from running away with the country. He also stressed, passionately and repeatedly, that it was essential for the people to understand the risks and benefits of government, to educate themselves, and to involve themselves in the political process. Without that, he said, the wolves will take over. Jefferson wrote: "Any nation that expects to be both ignorant and free expects what never was and never will be."

He advocated freedom of speech, in part so that even wildly unpopular views could be expressed, so that deviations from the conventional wisdom could be offered for consideration. Although personally an extremely amiable man, reluctant to criticize even his sworn enemies, he believed that the habit of skepticism is an important prerequisite for responsible citizenship. He argued that the cost of education is trivial compared to the cost of ignorance, of leaving the government to the wolves. He taught that the country is safe only when the people rule.

Part of the duty of citizenship is not to be intimidated into conformity. I wish that the oath of citizenship that you are about to take included something like "I promise to question everything my leaders tell me." That would be really to Thomas Jefferson's point. "I promise to use my critical faculties. I promise to develop my independence of thought. I promise to educate myself so I can make independent judgments." Even if they're not part of the official oath, you can nevertheless make such promises, silently, to yourself. That, it seems to me, would be a gift from you to your new country.

I also wish that the Pledge of Allegiance was directed at the Constitution and the Bill of Rights, as it is when the President takes his oath of office, rather than to the flag and the nation, as it is in all those other countries where the wolves are still in charge.

There is one other point I want to make. It comes to mind naturally in an election year, and in thinking about Jefferson and his colleagues. When we consider those founders of our nation, Jefferson, Washington, Samuel and John Adams, Madison and Monroe, both of whom lived down the road from Monticello, Benjamin Franklin, Tom Paine, there is a list of at least ten and maybe even dozens of great political leaders. They were well-educated. They were students of history. They knew human fallibility and weakness and corruptibility. They were fluent in the English language. They wrote their own speeches. They were realistic and practical, and at the same time motivated by high principles. They were not checking the pollsters on what to think this week. They knew what to think. They were comfortable with long-term thinking, planning even further ahead than the next election. They were true leaders. They were able to bring out the best in us. They attempted to set a course for our nation into the far future, not so much by establishing laws as by setting limits on what kinds of laws could be passed. The Constitution and its Bill of Rights have done remarkably well, constituting, despite human weaknesses, a machine able, more often than not, to correct its own trajectory.

At that time, there were only about two and a half million people in the United States. Today there are some two hundred and fifty million, a hundred times more. So if there were ten people of the caliber of Thomas Jefferson then, there ought to be $10 \times 100 = 1000$ Thomas Jeffersons today.

Where are they? We need them.

Of course, different times bring out different capabilities, and attract the talents of the American people into different walks of life. One of our chief obligations is to make a society that helps to mold and guide the people so we use our talents, and the best that is in us, for the common good, so we are committed to justice, so we are passionately engaged in the political process.

I suggest therefore that there is a second gift that you can give to the United States in return for the blessing of citizenship: for you and your children to work to encourage the Thomas Jeffersons (of both sexes) who must be among us, and to elicit the Thomas Jefferson in each of us.

I congratulate you on the step you take this day and welcome you to citizenship in the United States of America.

MEETING THE CHALLENGES IN EDUCATION

THE UNIVERSITY AND THE PUBLIC[1]
HUNTER R. RAWLINGS III[2]

During 1992 and 1993, colleges and universities throughout the country sought to come to grips with the problems created by diminished financial support for both public and private institutions. Reporting on a conference of presidents of more than 450 schools called to discuss the future of higher education, Anthony DePalma described the situation as follows:

> Tough economic times are forcing so many colleges and universities across the country to cut costs and adjust their ambitions that the shape of higher education may be significantly changed as the 21st century dawns. . . . The cuts at most universities would be so severe that they would reach deep into classrooms and research laboratories, challenging the institutions' commitment to excellence, yet presenting both opportunities as well as obstacles.
>
> Students and scholars in 2001 are likely to see large research universities like Yale and Columbia shrink and become more specialized, experts say. Teachers at elite private institutions and state-supported ones alike will be handling more courses. Tuition will be substantially higher and financial aid scarcer. This combination will push a college degree further out of reach for high school students from poor minority families, whose ranks will have grown faster than those of white students from middle-income families. (*New York Times*, February 3, 1992, p. 1)

Reinforcing DePalma's analysis were statistics from a study by the Center for Higher Education at Illinois State University showing that state appropriations for higher education in 1992 were lower than those of two years earlier. This is the first two-year drop in the country's history, exceeding even the cuts during the depression of the 1930s. Edward R. Hines, a professor of educational administration at Illinois State, where the study had been conducted, described the figures as "pretty shocking" and said that the bleak state budget picture would lead to a fundamental reshaping of higher education with state lawmakers and educa-

[1]Delivered to a university convocation, University of Iowa, Iowa City, Iowa, at 7:30 P.M. on September 24, 1992.
[2]For biographical note, see Appendix.

tors debating how best to reallocate existing funds, eliminate academic programs, and define workable missions for colleges. (Scott Jaschik, *The Chronicle of Higher Education*, October 21, 1992, p. A21)

Hunter R. Rawlings III, President of the University of Iowa, is one of many educators who seeks to prepare his institution, its scholars, administrators, and students, for changes that might come because of the new frugality.

Hunter Rawlings's speech: This is the year of the Angry American: the whole country is in a negative mood, and that includes Iowa. The upcoming elections have focused underlying resentment upon public officials and public institutions. All across the country, you hear the same refrain: "We can't afford everything; we're taxed to the hilt; we have too many public employees." In our own case, the refrain runs this way: "Why are our universities always complaining? They're better off than most of us; why can't they do a better job with what they have?"

From our perspective, things look very different: our costs are going up, state support for our operating budget is shrinking, our funds for travel and equipment have been cut—so for us, this is shaping up as the year of a faculty on the defensive and an overextended staff. As we struggle to hold onto the gains in quality we have worked so hard to achieve, here's what we feel like saying to our fellow Iowans: "We are working harder than ever before, producing more, generating a greater share of our own support; our research is winning the respect of our national and international colleagues; our students are getting the courses they need; we are providing a wide array of important services to the public. So why aren't we better appreciated here in our own state?"

The University and the state are sending each other strong messages, but something is being lost in transmission. We are not hearing each other as clearly as we need to. Tonight I want to be an amplifier for voices from both sides, in the hope of bringing us closer together, close enough, at least, to have a fruitful conversation.

I spend a great deal of my time on the road—always under the speed limit, I assure you, in spite of what you may have heard from people who ride with me—and most of my trips include talks to civic groups, business leaders, and public schools. At the end of these events I always take questions from the floor, and I learn a lot from these sessions. I also learn by visiting alumni groups, and by seeing students in my office, in class, and in the residence halls. I receive torrents of mail about every University activity you can imagine, and I've been interviewed by most of the major media outlets in the state. So I think I know how our constituents feel about The University of Iowa.

I am constantly impressed with how deeply the University is respected by the people of Iowa—held in awe, really—as a center of learning and culture. But there is a persistent undercurrent of negativity as well. Paradoxically, our very successes have generated a certain resentment around the state. Our size, our cosmopolitan character, and our large concentration of resources tend to isolate us somewhat from our fellow citizens. Especially in difficult economic times, we are perceived as an oasis of prosperity and privilege, remote from the lives of ordinary Iowans.

We shouldn't be surprised at this perception: we are a large institution in a thriving community, located 60 miles from the eastern border of an agricultural state of fewer than 3 million people, with more than 60 percent living in communities of less than 20,000. We tend to live in our own world, and many of us have insufficient appreciation of the culture of the small towns and rural communities from which we draw students.

So if we don't know Iowa, how can we expect Iowa to know us? How can we expect a farming family in Benton County, a tractor dealer in Fort Dodge, a grocer in Oelwein—people who have their own problems to worry about—to put themselves in our shoes? Or concern themselves with the effort we expend in keeping up with the rapid advance of knowledge, the intensive preparation required for college-level teaching, our long hours of one-to-one advising and counseling, the weekends consumed in writing comments on papers and dissertations? Even our own students don't always appreciate what it takes to bring new knowledge into the world—to develop a flash of insight into a fully funded research project or a completed scholarly publication or a brilliantly realized artistic creation. This is hard work, and not everyone can do it, but that doesn't mean that its value to society is always self-evident.

It's not just unfamiliarity with our work that generates criticism of the University. Some complaints are born of what we might call consumer frustration—annoyance at inconvenient or unobserved office hours, intimidating bureaucratic procedures, delays in responding to requests—things that appear within our ability to control.

Here are the three questions I am most often asked on the road (not counting the one about who's going to win next weekend):

1. Why doesn't my daughter ever see any of those world-renowned faculty members you're always talking about?

2. Why are your salaries so high, compared to everyone else's? (Here let me just comment that the median salary in Iowa is $17,505, below the halfway point nationally.)

3. All that research and economic development you generate may be fine for Iowa City, but what is the University doing for us in rural Iowa?

That's what people ask me off campus. Now let me tell you the top three questions I'm getting on campus this year, from all of you:

1. Why are we being insulted with directives to increase our "productivity"? We're already productive! We work 50 to 60 hours a week, and we get results. We're overburdened as it is: why make developmental assignments harder to get and load on more teaching hours, slowing down our research progress?

2. Why should anyone resent my earning a competitive salary, based on my value in the nationwide marketplace, given my long years of study and experience, and the expertise I'm making available to those who seek it?

3. Why do people question the University's involvement in research—when we are finding cures for diseases, publishing successful new books, and contributing to economic development in Iowa?

I hear what you're saying, and I'm sympathetic to it. But not everyone outside the University understands how much we have changed over the years, or why. We are not the same kind of institution we were 25 years ago: we're bigger, more nationally visible, and, like other universities of our stature, we have a number of important missions beyond undergraduate teaching.

Our emphasis has shifted to research and clinical care, in part because that's the sector of the University that has presented our best opportunity for growth and success. And in the heady eighties, when we began touting our achievements in terms of grants received and external dollars attracted to the state, the farm crisis deepened and rural communities began to lose their livelihood.

To many Iowans, understandably, The University of Iowa began to seem like a far-off dynamo of local success, insulated from the problems of the rest of the state. The result has been a deepening lack of understanding on both sides.

Inevitably, the more money a state university obtains from federal agencies, corporate foundations, and private donors, the less, in proportion, is the state's sense of "ownership" in the institution it has created. This is the phenomenon that law school Dean, Mark Yodof of the University of Texas, has called "the privatization of public universities." Yodof notes that "the inclusion of massive external subsidies gives the appearance that state university budgets are growing," even when the proportion of income from state sources is declining.

To the public, as Yodof observes, a larger overall university budget "gives a false sense of security and a false sense that no harm has been done," while in actuality the "new resources are benefiting only some parts of the university and not others." As Yodof writes, "It is as if every state university is really two universities, one reasonably funded and the other neglected." People on the street may wonder why we can't solve this problem by mixing state and non-state monies and spreading the resources around, but of course external grant funds are earmarked for specific purposes, purposes that don't, ordinarily, include undergraduate education.

This process of privatization has gone on for at least 40 years and is now probably irreversible. The states are now required to bear a greater proportion of the cost of federal social programs than they once did, and soaring health care costs are crowding out higher education and consuming whatever discretionary revenues they are able to raise. We are going to have to learn to live with these facts.

It is time, then, for us to begin working out a new compact with society. But the terms will not be easy. Here are the salient points that will figure in the negotiation:

First, there is an increasing public reluctance to regard higher education as sacrosanct, when it comes to cuts in public spending. This is part of a general tendency to question all publicly funded social services, including education, in the face of rising costs and competing human needs. It is no longer taken for granted that higher education is a good in itself, or that the excellence we seek is ours by right, a public entitlement.

Second, as I am sure you have observed, there is mounting public skepticism about the overall effectiveness of universities, as they are now constituted, in discharging their responsibilities. This skepticism has been fueled by the explosion of public interest in things like scientific fraud, price fixing, indirect cost abuse, out-of-control athletic programs, graduates who lack basic skills, and so on down the list. There is now a greater demand for "accountability" at all levels of education, from kindergarten through graduate and professional schools—and the bottom line is: how well is the faculty teaching our kids?

Third, our cities are in crisis; our K-12 system is in trouble; our national debt is out of hand. Where is the country to turn for help? One place is to universities, which despite their problems are among the strongest and most successful organizations we have in this country. And if we don't help, the effects will reach us eventually: unless the nationwide problems of K-12 education are alleviated soon, for example, the students who come here are going to be incapable of absorbing what we have to offer. In the post-Cold War era, we must prepare to offer the nation new kinds of assistance, services perhaps less prestigious than multimillion dollar research projects, but nonetheless essential for the health and stability of the kind of country we all want to live in.

I believe we will thrive in the future only if we cultivate and reinvigorate our deep roots as a service institution. This doesn't mean we should stop what we are doing now and do something else. Far be it from a classical philologist like me to derogate non-utilitarian scholarship! That kind of research is essential to what many of us do. But we can shift our focus slightly and make some subtle adjustments of attitude and ethos, remembering that our interdependent responsibilities in teaching, research, and service have a common origin as instruments of public good. As we know, universities did not come into existence for their own internal purposes. The University of Iowa, like all state universities, was created to serve the people, or, as the founding legislation of 1847 phrases it in a narrower context: to provide what "the public convenience may hereafter require."

Teaching, research, and public service, are all, in their way, avenues for extending our resources to others.

To nourish our roots in service, we need to ensure that everything we undertake is imbued with the ethic of our founding traditions. This applies not only to the public outreach programs that are normally classified in the "service" category, but also to our research and teaching, which at a public university are in themselves means of public service.

Our service takes so many forms and emanates from so many different sources within the University that we ourselves don't always realize how much of it we are performing or give ourselves enough credit for doing it. But let me give you just a few examples of the kinds of services we are providing—examples that can easily be multiplied:

We are strengthening education in Iowa at all levels, across a wide expanse of disciplines. We have recently received a grant from the Howard Hughes Medical Institute that will help us do a better job of attracting young people into science in high school and college. Winning a new generation to science is, in some ways, even more difficult than solving scientific problems ourselves, but it is a service very much needed in our state and our nation.

Just two weeks ago, our program in Literature, Science, and the Arts received word that it has won a U.S. Department of Education grant to develop a curriculum in Ethics, Risk, Decision-Making, and Public Policy, in collaboration with Iowa State University and nearby colleges. Our Japanese faculty and the Center for Asian and Pacific Studies have worked with the state's foreign language commission to help high schools launch 10 fledgling programs in Japanese—from Mason City to Clarinda, from Council Bluffs to Davenport.

Our creative and performing artists also provide services to the state—just look at what one novel from the Writers' Workshop has done for the tourist industry in Dyersville! The driveway around Hancher Auditorium is often filled with yellow buses while schoolchildren attend special performances, and we have recently started a program that introduces third-graders to our Museum of Art. And faculty artists, musicians, dancers, and writers conduct performances and master classes around the state.

To find out what else we are doing for Iowans, Kate Gfeller recently conducted a Faculty Senate survey, and I'll just give a very few examples from the long list she has compiled. A professor in the College of Business Administration and her doctoral student are studying how grain producers make selling decisions and are disseminating the information they have gathered on the role of farm women through the Farm Women's Forum. Professors in the College of Law help draft legislation and provide *pro bono* legal services to indigents. A professor in the College of Education has helped organize a grant proposal to the National Science Foundation for a statewide program to improve instruction in mathematics. A professor with a joint appointment in Geography and Civil and Environmental Engineering has assessed ground water quality in Iowa. Professor Gfeller herself serves as a resource in music therapy to music educators and special education staff around the state.

Our best-known service to the state is of course the contribution our health science colleges and The University of Iowa Hospitals and Clinics make to the health of Iowans. We are national leaders in educating primary-care physicians for service in small towns and rural communities. Our Family Practice Preceptorship Program, which is required of all third-year medical students, pairs students with family practice mentors at 130 locations around the state, and our Office of Community-Based Programs has helped more than 50 Iowa communities attract doctors, just in the last year and a half. Our Institute of Agricultural Medicine and Occupational Health is testing interior air quality in workplaces, and the Iowa Center for Agricultural Safety and Health, a collaborative project with Iowa State University, is providing comprehensive services to Iowa farm families to reduce or eliminate hazards. And our specialists in cardiology are bringing their services closer to the people who need them by operating satellite care stations in Ottumwa, Keosauqua, and Muscatine.

We are also improving the service we offer to Iowans in the form of teaching, mainly by increasing opportunities for undergraduates to study with our permanent faculty. Increased involvement of professors in undergraduate teaching has become a national trend in higher education, prompted partly by economic necessity, partly by our own recognition that the three components of our mission have slipped out of balance.

Public pressures for redressing the balance are intensifying. Scarcely a week goes by without some national study or prominent editorial deploring low undergraduate teaching loads at research universities, and arguing that respect for teaching is at an all-time low. Last week the Select Committee on Children, Youth, and Families of the House of Representatives held hearings on faculty workloads, and legislators in Arizona, Missouri, Ohio, Virginia, and Rhode Island are engaged in similar investigations.

These public pressures can only increase. If we don't deal with the linked issues of undergraduate teaching and faculty workloads ourselves, we are likely to have someone else's idea of a solution imposed upon us from outside.

News articles on this matter reveal appalling misunderstandings of the nature of our work and the purposes of a research university. A recent piece in the *Chicago Tribune* quotes someone who suggests that if the faculty were to teach more, then "graduate students would be largely unnecessary"—as if future professors will spring fully-formed from the head of Zeus. A state auditor in North Carolina questions whether the description of a professor's work should include such activities as "reading professional magazines, consulting with colleagues, . . . [and] 'thinking'," as if someone who avoids such things might be even minimally capable of teaching in college.

We are not going to let misconceptions like these dictate discussion of faculty workloads at The University of Iowa. We are conducting our own reassessment. As has been widely reported this fall, a committee of faculty members and administrators has been working with Vice President Nathan on a Framework for Instructional Improvement for The University of Iowa. In July the committee submitted its recommendations to the Board of Regents. Now deans, department heads, and faculty members are working on plans that will be presented to the Board of Regents in December and will go into effect in the spring semester.

Among other provisions, such as devising better ways of assessing teaching effectiveness and augmenting incentives for excellent teaching, we will be adjusting the balance between teaching and research on an individual and departmental basis. These adjustments will increase opportunities, over all, for undergraduates to take courses with members of our permanent faculty.

Under the new plan, we will also offer some of our low-enrollment courses less frequently, at both graduate and undergraduate levels, and combine, phase out, or discontinue other undersubscribed courses. And we will look more closely at faculty developmental assignments, to ensure that these semesters away from teaching will not reduce the availability of essential courses to students, and to make sure that the released time directly enhances the faculty member's future achievement in scholarship and teaching.

I've been talking tonight mostly about adjustments affecting the faculty. But before I close, I want to say a special word of appreciation for the services provided to the rest of us by our hard-working staff. Our staff members, whether they hold professional and scientific or support positions, know all about service, especially in this last year, after we lost 480 positions, and they could teach the rest of us a great deal. By the very nature of their work, many staff members work behind the scenes. With unassuming effectiveness, they anticipate the needs of the faculty and students—and render the essential services that keep the University going. They deserve our thanks and recognition.

These are unsettling times in higher education. Sixty percent of all colleges and universities in the country had their operating budgets cut last year. For those of us who developed our expectations for public support of higher education in the expansive sixties—a period of very different social needs and spending priorities—adjustment to a different reality is hard.

It does not help matters when public officials lambaste hardworking state employees, including us, and fail to acknowledge the extraordinary contributions we make to the state.

But cherishing the feeling that we are undervalued and unappreciated doesn't help matters, either. The best way for us to win the state's support in tight times is to listen with sensitivity and understanding to the views of our fellow citizens, and, in turn, to educate them about the work we do here. We are one of the most successful and influential institutions in Iowa. The state needs us badly. If we can shift our balance slightly and infuse an ethic of service into everything we do, we will have gone a long way toward bringing the University and the public back together.

NATIONAL SECURITY: CHILDREN, CRIME, AND CITIES[1]
D. STANLEY EITZEN[2]

Dr. D. Stanley Eitzen, Professor of Sociology at Colorado State University, was the 1992 Scholar in Residence at Hanover College in Hanover, Indiana. Hanover, a small, private, coeducational, liberal arts college, affiliated with the Presbyterian church, annually invites a recognized scholar to visit the campus, lecture, meet with faculty and students and participate in classroom activities and informal discussion.

During his week-long visit to Hanover College in mid-October of 1992, Dr. Eitzen delivered three major lectures. The title of his second public lecture is "National Security: Crime, Cities and Children." Early in the speech he explains that the term "national security" usually refers to the defensibility of our national border

[1]Delivered to a university convocation, at Fitzgibbon Recital Hall, Hanover College, Hanover, Indiana, at 7:30 P.M. on October 14, 1992.
[2]For biographical note, see Appendix.

and the protection of the country's interests abroad. Acknowledging that external threats to our country still exist, Eitzen contends that since the collapse of the communism and the end of the cold war, serious domestic problems have emerged as the chief threats to the national security, namely—the plight of poor children, crime, and the decay of our cities.

Eitzen delivered this lecture to a convocation in Fitzgibbon Recital Hall in the Center for Fine Arts at 7:30 P.M. on October 14, 1992. His audience of close to 100 people included students, faculty and townspeople. This address was later reprinted in *Vital Speeches of the Day.*

D. Stanley Eitzen's speech: Let me begin with a "truth in advertising" disclaimer. I am not a dispassionate observer of social life. My biases will be clearly evident in my analysis this evening. In part these biases are personal. I am a social democrat. I favor democracy, equality of opportunity, and reducing inequality so that the disadvantaged have a decent minimum of food, shelter, and health care. My biases also reflect my discipline, sociology, which requires the critical analysis of social arrangements. We sociologists must ask continually: how does the system work and who benefits and who does not from the way it works?

Now I realize that these biases place me in some jeopardy. This is Republican country—Dan Quayle country for heaven's sake. I am reminded of the question asked by comedian George Gobel, who was popular 35 years ago. He asked: "Did you ever think that the world was a tuxedo and you were a pair of *brown* shoes?" Well, perhaps I am a pair of brown shoes in your tuxedo world. But I ask you to hear me out. I believe that what I have to say is *not* being said in the current political campaign and rarely by our political leaders. Yet we ought to confront these domestic problems or we are all in trouble, Republicans and Democrats, conservatives and liberals.

I want to address *national security.* This term typically refers to securing our borders from invaders and protecting our interests abroad. It requires planning ahead, manufacturing the necessary military hardware, deploying personnel to the right places, and spending whatever it takes. Our political leaders use the flag, patriotism, and slogans such as protecting the "American Way of Life" to inspire us to sacrifice to do whatever is necessary, whether it is preparing for war, rationing, or higher taxes for *national security.* And, typically, we respond with enthusiasm because our *national security* is the "highest calling" of citizens.

Well, the Cold War is over. We spent many trillions of dollars since World War II in our competition with the Soviet Union, as they did, and we, apparently, won. The Soviet Union has broken up, as has its network of satellites. Soviet communism is vastly diminished, found in one form or another only in Cuba, North Korea, and China.

Despite the demise of Soviet communism our national security remains in jeopardy. There are several external threats such as our dependence on foreign oil, the existence of outlaw governments, acts of terrorism, as well as global warming, the depletion of the ozone layer, and the destruction of the tropical rain forests. These external threats are important but so, too, are domestic problems. I want to focus on three domestic issues that threaten our security: the plight of poor children, rising street crime, and the decay of our cities.

Children are the most seriously disadvantaged age group in the United States. Several facts show the magnitude of the problem of disadvantaged children:

—Twenty-two percent of U.S. children under 18 live *below* the poverty line. About one-half of black children under 18 live below the poverty line.

Eight hundred thousand children are homeless.

One out of 8 children under age 12 are hungry.

About one-third of all pregnant women receive insufficient prenatal health care.

About 20 nations have a lower infant mortality rate than the U.S. The black infant mortality rate is twice that for whites.

The outlook for poor children is grim. Because they were born to disadvantaged parents they are denied, for the most part, the building blocks of early development: adequate nutrition, decent medical care, and a safe and secure environment. As a result, by age 5 or so, they will be less alert, less curious, and less effective at interacting with their peers than more privileged children. Thus, they begin school already behind. Moreover, they will likely attend the most poorly staffed, overcrowded, and ill-equipped schools. To summarize, poor children are more likely than more advantaged children: to have health problems, to not do well in school (to be truant, troublesome, and to drop out), to be in trouble with law, and, as adults to be unwed parents, unemployed, and on welfare. In short, many of these poor children will always be a problem, and a costly problem, at that, for society.

Society is not meeting the needs of these children. Three examples make this point: (1) Currently, less than 5 percent of the federal budget goes to programs to benefit children. This is in sharp contrast to those federal programs for those 65 and older, which receive five times as much. (2) The U.S. is the only Western society without some form of universal health care. (3) Only about one in four children who qualify for Head Start receive it.

One answer is to have the states provide programs for their children. This solution is flawed because states vary in their resources and in their willingness to fund programs for the disadvantaged.

The irony is that as a society we will spend whatever it takes to buy weapons systems, spending, for example, almost $1 billion per stealth bomber because weapons are needed for national security. Moreover, even fiscally-strapped states will give a high priority to building and maintaining prisons because they are also needed for security. In California, which is experiencing difficult financial times, the 1991 budget for prison increased by 11 percent, while the budget for Aid to Families with Dependent Children was cut by 9 percent. Most significant, 11 states spent 24 times more on prisons than on child care and child development programs.

Our relative abandonment of poor children increases the likelihood that they will not do well in school, and that many will engage in criminal behaviors. Some facts:

The rate of violent crime by juveniles is up more than 25 percent in the last 10 years.

Black youths are being arrested for violent crimes at a rate five times that for white youths.

In the past decade there has been a 79 percent increase in the number of juveniles committing murder with guns.

The conservative response to these trends is more: more police, more judges, and more prisons. Conservatives have sought and received from legislatures mandatory and harsher sentences. There are three fundamental criticisms of this solution by progressives. First, this get-tough philosophy has not worked. The U.S. incarceration rate is 426 per 100,000, the highest in the industrialized world yet the crime rate continues to increase. Our incarceration rate is *triple* that of the United Kingdom, our closest Western European competition, and 10 times greater than that found in the Netherlands. The second problem with the conservative solution is that it is an "after-the-fact" solution. That is, it attacks crime and criminals rather than the sources of anti-social acts. Third, there is a fundamental contradiction in the conservative solution because it seeks to build up the criminal justice system while reducing or dismantling the social justice system. By my logic, this tries to fight crime by sustaining and even enhancing a criminogenic climate. In doing so, of course, we are less safe.

The progressive solution is opposite the current strategy. Instead of "after-the-fact" efforts, we need a sustained effort to build up a comprehensive social justice system, which is "before-the-fact" of criminal behavior. At a minimum, this requires programs that focus on several areas. First, families must be strengthened. Single-parent families and the working poor need subsidized child care, flexible work schedules, and leave for family emergencies. Adolescent parents need the resources to stay in school. They also need parenting classes and job training. Second, there must be a societal commitment to full and decent employment. Adults need jobs, jobs that pay more than the minimum wage. Jobs promote stability. People get married and they are more likely to stay married if they have an adequate and stable economic situation. Third, increased public services must be provided to those now stripped of economic security. This means the provision of a universal and comprehensive health care system, low-cost housing, job training, and the generous spending for schools in low-income areas.

If we do not provide these social justice measures, then we can continue to watch the downward spiral of the disadvantaged, which will make our streets and lives less and less secure.

Poor children and street crimes are concentrated in our declining cities. No other major industrial society has allowed its cities to face the fiscal and social troubles that confront the cities of the United States. Five trends had led to these problems.

The first trend has been the suburban exodus that has occurred since World War II. This has meant that affluent families left the city to live in affluent enclaves, while the city lost their tax revenues.

The cities also lost financially because of the second trend, corporate flight. Businesses, many of which hired workers at relatively high wages, fled U.S. cities for more favorable business climates in the suburbs, rural areas, the South, and Third World countries. This meant that cities lost thousands and thousands of jobs that paid middle-class wages and benefits.

The cities have also been drained economically because their inhabitants *send* more to the military in taxes than the cities and people *receive* from military contracts, salaries, and facilities. In

Los Angeles in 1990, for example, taxpayers sent $4.74 billion to the Pentagon yet received only $1.47 billion for a net loss of $3.27 billion (which is the equivalent of about 100,000 jobs).

A fourth economic drain that hurts cities is redlining. This is the practice of banks and other lending institutions to deny loans to home buyers and small business entrepreneurs in cities, especially the poor districts in cities. Redlining creates a self-fulfilling prophecy as banks refuse to loan in certain areas because they are assumed to be high credit risk areas. The lack of money results in the failure of businesses and falling property values, which justifies further redlining.

Finally, federal monies to the cities were slashed under Presidents Reagan and Bush. Overall, since 1980 federal spending to the cities *declined* by 60 percent, eliminating revenue sharing and cutting programs such as public works, economic development, job training, health and nutrition, schools, and housing.

These trends, taken together, have had severe consequences for cities and their inhabitants, especially the poor. The cities have had to downsize their operations such as road maintenance, and police and fire protection. Health and housing codes have been neglected. The shrinking inventory of low-cost housing combined with the increasing number of people at economic risk have increased the numbers of homeless dramatically. City health services cannot meet the growing demand of the poor who have no medical insurance. Furthermore, as Jonathan Kozol has described in *Savage Inequalities*, the cities have much less money for their schools than do suburban schools. The irony, of course, is that inner city children have greater needs than suburban children. Finally, the cities serve as the nation's poorhouses, containing a disproportionate share of the dependent population (the poor, unemployed, elderly, homeless, and AIDS victims).

At a time when the cities face a worsening fiscal crisis and a growing number of problems, they are losing their political clout. The 1992 election, for example, is the first time when more than 50 percent of the voters lived in the suburbs. This explains why the presidential candidates avoided the problems of the cities.

Will the abandonment of the cities continue? If we do so, we will not be safer.

The solution to the problems I have raised do not require changing bad people. They require changing bad social policy. Our politicians either do not have the wisdom or the courage to attack these problems. But we, too, are to blame. The comfortable are sheltered for the most part from the problems of poverty, crime, and decaying cities. But we, all of us, must be willing to sacrifice to solve these problems as if we were in a national emergency. We must do this because it is in our interest—our national interest, or national security, if you will—to work out solutions to these problems and pay whatever the price just as in wartime. To do otherwise, insures a declining and less secure America.

SHAPING THE FUTURE

SAVING OUR CITIES[1]
TOM GERETY[2]

The 1992 Trinity College graduating seniors, together with their families, friends and faculty, listened to three speeches on commencement day—May 17, 1992. At the morning baccalaureate exercises, Stephen Charleston, the native American Episcopal Bishop of the Alaskan Diocese and graduate of Trinity, preached about the impact and legacy of Christopher Columbus's arrival in North America. Later that afternoon, Irish poet Brendon Kennelly delivered the principal commencement address on the importance of education. The third speaker was the president of Trinity, Tom Gerety, who spoke to the 1992 graduates on the plight of American cities and why many people choose not to live and work in them.

Three speeches on such diverse themes illustrate a fairly recent development in public address—the use of commencement exercises as a forum for the discussion of significant public questions. While all three speeches received local press coverage, President Gerety's charge was excerpted by the national publication *The Chronicle of Higher Education.* Gerety, who has four degrees from Yale, including a doctor of laws, as well as a master and doctor of philosophy, was named president of Trinity College less than three years before. This appointment followed a career teaching law, ethics, and political philosophy at the universities of Pittsburgh, Stanford and Indiana.

In this address, Gerety speaks of the transformation of American cities that has occurred in the last quarter-century. He focusses on the broad implications that the decline of our cities will have for the entire country.

Approximately 2,000 attended the graduation exercises, which were held outdoors on the quadrangle, a rectangle of green grass with ash trees shading its center, bordered by collegi-

[1]Delivered at the Trinity College commencement, Hartford, Connecticut, at 2:00 P.M. on May 17, 1992.
[2]For biographical note, see Appendix.

ate Gothic buildings. Preceding Gerety's address was the commencement address by Kennelly, presentation of the Brownell prize in teaching, remarks by the senior class president and the conferring of 477 bachelors, 34 masters and 9 honorary degrees.

Tom Gerety's speech: I grew up in the country, or what seemed to me the country. We had fields all around our house, with woods beyond them. In the spring, Mr. Ference came with his tractor to turn the ground and plant rows of corn and potatoes. All summer we would hide in the cornrows or make our way through them to their mysterious honeysuckled borders, near the stonewall at the edge of the woods. Three giant maples stood astride the fields, perhaps a quarter mile back from our yard.

To me the country meant solitude: there was no one to play with except my own brothers. Across the street from us lived Newton Hawkins and his sister, an ancient pair in an ancient house. Because of his name, I will forever associate them with the invention and production of what to me was the most exquisite delicacy of my childhood, the fig newton. They drew their water from a well and had no plumbing. They were reported to be the last of their line; they and their ancestors farmed land that, over two centuries, had been sold down to less than an acre.

On holidays we always went to the city. New York City was to me, in those first few years after the second world war, a splendid if somewhat daunting gathering of people, places, zoos, skyscrapers, museums and shops. My immigrant grandparents lived there with hot pretzels and strong brogues and close neighbors.

All my life I have loved cities, loved them as only a child of the country can love them, as a convert, a yearner, a dreamer for whom they live partly in fantasy and ideal. As soon as I could get away from the country, I did: to Paris for the last year of high school, to Lima, Peru, for one year of college, to New Haven and Chicago and Pittsburgh and Cincinnati—and now to Hartford. Cities have always held out to me the promise, even in their sounds and smells, of adventure, of ideas, of music and art, of markets and conversation.

Few of us can be blessed with the wisdom to know more than a portion of what really goes on around us. Was it Hegel who said that what is familiar is what is hardest to see and understand? For children, time meanders among a few landmarks: the corner store, the playground, the walk or ride to school. Later, time rushes by, or seems to, no longer a rivulet but a river.

Coming back to Connecticut after years away, I had the impression, on Hartford's streets, that little had changed: the three-family houses on Crescent and Broad, the kids in the doorways, the bustle of commuters downtown; this looked to me like New Haven or Bridgeport twenty years before when I was still a student.

But in my lifetime, and in yours, a great shift has taken place in the life of cities.

My father and mother moved to the country to rear a family in green and quiet, near woods and fields. But my father was no country-person; he was a new variety of American: a suburbanite. He commuted by train to the city; all over the United States (and a little later over much of Europe) commuters in cars and trains were building houses farther and farther from the great centers of work and culture. Soon the farms began to disappear; both the Hawkins died; Mr. Ference no longer baled hay in the heat at the end of summer.

Millions and millions of us have participated in this process of transformation. What one scholar has called the "crabgrass frontier" has lured us on as irresistibly as the Western frontier did in the 19th Century.

"First, the people went to the suburbs to live," someone said to me last year. "Then the shops went to the suburbs; and now the jobs are moving to the suburbs."

What I saw as a child was a lush countryside and an equally lush, if very different, city.

What I did not see—and what now we cannot fail to see—is that the America of suburbs leaves neither the countryside nor the cities intact. And plainly it is the cities that suffer most.

Several days after the riot in Los Angeles, commentators began to compare what had happened there with the riots of the late 1960s. The photographs showed what had become of neighborhoods and streets in Newark and Detroit and Chicago, burned out and vandalized a long time ago. With few exceptions, they remain now, a quarter-century later, just as they were in the days *after* their riots. Stores that were burnt down often do not reopen; houses rarely go up again in a neighborhood destroyed in a night.

What happened in Los Angeles, in anarchy and anger, is striking and vivid to us now, as it should be. But it should be no more vivid or striking than what we see around us in nearly every city in the nation.

Those who can choose where they will live or work are choosing too often *against* cities. The result, should we let this go on much longer, will be that our cities will die. In their place will rise up 'edge' cities, built up around monotonous succession of malls—for shopping, for work, for schooling, for housing, for entertainment, and, above all, for parking.

What we will lose should America lose its cities is incalculable. Some, like Jane Jacobs, the great champion of street-life, believe that without cities a nation can have no economic future. She argues from history: great cities bring together the skills and energy and markets that foster industry and invention.

It is a good argument. Still it may prove false; perhaps we can have a strong economy without strong cities.

There are even better arguments for saving our cities.

Whatever our economic future, our cultural future without cities is barren and meager. If somehow invention and industry survive without cities, will theaters and museums and symphonies? Cities provide the one ecological niche where human beings push themselves to greater and greater achievements not only in commerce but in all the arts, especially the highest and most complex.

Patriotism, too, requires of us a standard of national achievement. We cannot lose our pride in our cities without losing some measure of our pride in our nation. To say of this country that it will someday soon have no great cities, nothing to compare to Paris or Budapest, to Delhi or Cairo, is to say that we will have no settlements of cultural and economic stature to stand alongside those of other nations.

Finally, America's cities are the great integrators of our people, of the new immigrant from Laos, Haiti or Nicaragua along with the old immigrant from Poland or Italy, Ireland or England. Cities bring us together and teach us new ideas and new possibilities. They teach us to live with one another; they permit us to see close up what we all share of the human condition, of its virtues, its vices, and its variable genius for everything from baking to poetry.

When I look out on your future, leaving school as you do in a time of some uncertainty, I have no fear for you as individuals. You are a sturdy, bright, and tenacious class. If the world does not at first open its arms to you, it will, in time, if you persevere.

But I do fear for America. We seem as a nation to have fallen into cynicism and apathy; drift seems our only response to what ails us. On our urban frontiers we give way to a greater and greater divide between those who can make choices in their lives and those who cannot. In this direction lies an American South Africa, separated out into camps: to one side, the prosperous and choosing; to the other, those for whom there is no chance of prosperity and little to choose from. Our cities in this bleak vision will be the Sowetos of our South Africa: segregated, impoverished, disordered—and without much hope.

This need not happen; we have it in our power to stop it, you and I. *We* can call America to its senses and restore its pride in *all* its settlements.

I charge you, then, with the care of our cities and of their citizens. Athens, said Thucydides, was the teacher of Greece. Our cities, too, teach the glory and promise of America. In forsaking them we forsake the hope of our democracy.

IN TODAY WALKS TOMORROW[1]
RANDALL L. TOBIAS[2]

McDonough Caperton Insurance Group is a prominent West Virginia company affiliated with one of the nation's largest insurance brokers—American Business Insurance, Inc. Like many successful corporations, the company feels a responsibility to its clients, employees, stockholders and community. One way in which McDonough Caperton has sought to fulfill this obligation is by establishing a "Distinguished Lecture Series" at the University of West Virginia's College of Business and Economics. The series has two main objectives: to increase public understanding of the business and economic systems as well as the contributions and social responsibilities of business; and to supplement college programs as an educational resource and public service.

Twice a year the insurance group brings visiting lecturers to the university campus. On October 14, 1992, the speaker was Randall L. Tobias, vice-chairman of the board of AT&T and

---

[1]Delivered in the Business and Economics Building, University of West Virginia, Morgantown, West Virginia, at 3:30 P.M. on October 14, 1992.
[2]For biographical note, see Appendix.

chairman and chief executive officer of AT&T International. Early in his lecture, Tobias assures his audience that although his topic is concerned with technology, his address would not be a technical talk. He then discusses six major developments in communication that the audience can expect to see in the next decade. He also relates to his audience how these new technologies will affect our work, homes and leisure.

Mr. Tobias delivered his talk at 3:30 p.m., Wednesday, October 14, 1992 in an auditorium in the Business and Economics building, which is located on the downtown campus of the University of West Virginia at Morgantown. About 250 students, faculty, administrators and members of the community attended the lecture which was open to the public.

Randall L. Tobias's speech: It's a pleasure to be back at West Virginia University and an honor to be presenting the McDonough Caperton Lecture.

My topic today is shaping the future through technology. But it will not be a technical talk. My interest lies less in the technology itself, though I am fascinated by how it works. My interest is more in how technology can be used to benefit AT&T's customers.

The topic is a risky one because it touches on some of society's deepest hopes and fears. Our literature is filled with conflicting views of technology and the future, from Edward Bellamy's utopian "Looking Backward" to Aldous Huxley's bleak "Brave New World." We've been exposed enough to both extremes to regard technology as a promise and a threat.

A lighthearted story I heard from a scientist-colleague illustrates this point.

A theologian asked the most powerful supercomputer, "Is there a God?" The computer said it lacked the processing power to know. It asked to be connected to all the other supercomputers in the world. Still, it was not enough power. So the computer was hooked up to all the mainframes in the world, and then all the minicomputers, and then all the personal computers. And eventually it was connected to all the computers in cars, microwaves, VCRs, digital watches, and so on. The theologian asked for the final time, "Is there a God?" And the computer replied: "There is now."

I heard some nervousness in the laughter. Don't worry. I can assure you, with a tinge of regret, that the information industry is a long time away from that kind of computer connectivity. But I can report we are making rapid progress with computers that understand spoken language and answer in kind.

In fact, progress in communications and computer technology has become so rapid that as much as you've seen in the 1980s, you haven't seen anything yet. As John Scully, CEO of Apple, put it: "We've been racing to the starting line. The really interesting stuff begins in the 1990's."

The next decade or so we will see: computers that speak and understand spoken language; personal telephone numbers that allow you to be reached anywhere; pocket-size personal communicators that combine computer and communication technology; high definition TV and hundreds of cable channels; two-way videophones; and computerized virtual reality.

Today, I'll describe these remarkable devices and capabilities. I'll discuss them in the context of overcoming four limitations on communications: the limits of geography, mobility, sense perception, and the human-machine interface. And I'll comment on how over the decade communications technology will change our work, home, and leisure lives.

And when I'm done I hope you will agree with the British poet Samuel Coleridge who said, "In today, already walks tomorrow."

But first, let's ignore the warning label on the back of communications devices: you know, the one that says only qualified technicians should open. Let's figuratively remove the cover and peek inside at two underlying technologies: microelectronics and fiber optics, for these are the basic technologies driving communications "warp-speed" into the 21st century.

Foremost, is microelectronics: transistors and other electronic components etched on a sliver of silicon. Thanks to the small-is-beautiful movement in electronics, there are more microprocessors—that is, computers on a chip—than there are people on earth.

Over the last few decades, the rate of progress in microelectronics has been fantastic. The number of components on a chip has been doubling every 18 months, without a substantial cost increase. To put that in perspective, if we had similar gains in automotive technology, today you could buy a Lexus for about $2. It would travel at the speed of sound, and go 600 miles on a thimble of gas. It would be only three inches long, but easy to parallel park!

Today we can squeeze about 32 million transistors on a chip.

By the year 2000, we will shoehorn 256 million onto a chip, allowing us to pack the power of today's supercomputer on a desktop. By the year 2010, with a billion transistors on a chip, we will have exhausted the limits of the current technology. And we may well tap the ultra-small world of quantum physics. I'm told by our scientists at Bell Laboratories that quantum technology might permit chips with a trillion transistors.

While microelectronics has the raw power to process huge amounts of information, information only gains its full value when communicated. Enter fiber optics, the technology of communicating with light.

Fiber optics systems combine lasers as small as grains of sand with glass fibers as thin as strands of hair. Unlike ordinary glass, it's ultra-pure. If oceans were made of this glass, you could see to the bottom.

In fiber optic systems, lasers transmit billions of light pulses each second as bits of data through these glass strands. The bits represent conversations, computer data or images. Currently, we transmit about 3.4 billion bits a second, equal to 50,000 simultaneous phone calls on a pair of fibers. But with not-too-distant developments in the technology, we expect to transmit one trillion bits per second, of about 70 million simultaneous conversations on a single pair of fibers. Such advances in these well-matched technologies are helping us to overcome the limitations on communication.

First, geography. For the last hundred years, most of our effort has been in shrinking distance, making it as easy to call another continent as it is to call another state. And we've largely succeeded. We now have global networks that allow you to directly dial up not only Peoria and Paris but even remote Pitcairn Island where the Bounty's mutineers landed. There's virtually no country or territory a consumer can't reach, no market a business can't access by telephone.

These global networks have been a spur to the world economy. Fiber cables under the oceans have evolved into the new trade routes of a global economy that prizes information as the most precious of all cargos.

Using global networks, corporations are able to establish far-flung world operations. For example, today Mazda offers a sports model designed in California, financed in Tokyo, and assembled in Michigan and Mexico with advanced electronic components invented in New Jersey but fabricated in Japan. To say the least, it takes tight communication linkages worldwide to pull this off. And Mazda is but one of thousands of global companies doing it every day.

With international networks in place we can now tackle individual mobility. When people left their homes or offices, they used to be hard to reach. And if on the road traveling, impossible to reach. But that has changed with wireless technology, through-the-air communication.

It began with cellular phones that could allow you to, theoretically, carry on a running conversation as you drove from New York to LA. It gained even greater popularity with cordless phones at home and in business.

Over the decade, we'll cut the cord for good with affordable personal communication networks that operate on radio waves. People will have a personal telephone number for life and will be tracked as they move from one service area to another. You could be reached anywhere. Whether in a cab, walking on the street, or waiting on line in a supermarket. Whether in West Virginia, California, or on the European continent. But only if you want to be reached, as I'll explain shortly.

You will receive calls with "personal communications devices," or "pocket phones." More than just miniature phones, personal communicators could combine telephone service with computer technology such as electronic mail and facsimile. You will be able to easily store notes in these devices by writing with a special pen on a computer screen. I know it sounds futuristic. But, in fact personal communicators will hit the market this year.

You can imagine the impact devices will have on the way we do business. For example, if you can pack an office in a briefcase, or even in your pocket, do you need an office?

The answer was "no" for 500 AT&T salespeople in ten states. They traded their offices for car phones, portable computers, printers and modems that transmit data over the telephone lines. The results have been overwhelmingly positive, more direct contact with customers and higher productivity. We plan to extend the concept to thousands of other salespeople.

Communications mobility may force even more sweeping changes in the workplace. An estimated 5.5 million people "tele-commuted" in the U.S. last year, and we expect the number to double by 1995. Converging with home office technologies, social forces are putting pressure on companies to further expand work at home.

Traffic and pollution, for example. As more persons per household work, traffic gets worse. The average length of a commute is expected to double in the 1990s from about 37 minutes today to one hour and 15 minutes, and that's just one way. As car pollutants double and traffic jams increase, federal and local governments will pressure business to expand work at home.

The social ramifications of work-at-home are enormous. For example, people who telecommute could choose to live in remote, rural locations, though probably not too far from the office since occasional face-to-face meetings will still be required.

On the downside, working at home may cause social isolation, one reason why face-to-face meetings will still be a fairly frequent part of worklife. On the other hand, some people may overcome the isolation by becoming part of a "virtual community." People who have never met but have common interests may communicate regularly with each other over computer networks.

Of course, being on-call, anytime, anywhere has its drawbacks. But even as technology creates a privacy problem, it offers a solution. When you want to, you can choose not to answer and still get the message by directing the telephone network to take your calls, like having an answering machine constantly at your disposal. You can retrieve the messages at your convenience, from anywhere and in any form you want, whether voice, print or electronic mail.

Most of us don't think of a telephone conversation as unnatural communication, but in a way it is. People prefer to see people when they talk. It adds an extra dimension of feeling and understanding. Conventional telephone service is an unnatural separation of our senses of sight and sound.

But we're working on bringing them back together again. Indeed, visual communication may well be to telecommunication in this decade what facsimile was in the '80s, an explosive technology.

Video communication used to require an expensive investment in equipment. Moving images eat up an enormous amount of telecommunications capacity. But scientists have developed compression techniques, a bit like the electronic equivalent of concentrated orange juice, that remove much of the visual information for transmission and restore it at the receiving end to constitute the picture.

As a result, AT&T has just introduced affordable videophones that use the standard telephone lines. The response has been so great we already have thousands on back order. Who is buying them? People with particularly strong incentive to see their family or friends. For example, grandparents who live far from their grandchildren and want to be able to see them grow up. Or parents sending children off to college who want to lessen the sense of separation and at the same time nervously monitor changes in hair and clothing styles.

Video will really take off in the mid-to-late 1990s when high-definition television, or HDTV, hits the market. High-definition television uses twice as many lines as standard television to create a moving image, in essence doubling the clarity. An HDTV picture has the color and the crispness of a 35 millimeter slide and the sound of a compact disc. Because the image is so well defined, it's possible to make larger TV screens without degrading the image quality. And, with digital technology, it's possible to get special effects, like zooming in on the pass receiver during a football game.

Over the decade, too, public demand for more video channels likely will prompt local cable or telephone companies to begin installing high capacity fiber optics to the home. Then 150 channels, and the potential for 10 times more, will be possible. And your TV guide may weigh as much as your telephone directory.

Within the next 20 years, we'll move beyond sight and sound with "virtual reality." Virtual reality uses specially designed goggles and gloves with computer chips embedded in them and communicates directly to a computer with radio transmitters. It can give the user the impression of being in a particular setting. The user's hand and eye movements are detected and the scene is moved to create the perspective being looked at. Not only is there dimensional perspective possible, but also the sense of motion and even smell.

At first blush, this might seem a trivial technology with sensational entertainment value only, an attraction in a pinball arcade. But virtual reality may prove to be practical.

For example, you may have heard about the murder trial in California where a video tape using virtual reality techniques was used to reenact the crime. In a less sensational illustration, Chrysler engineers have been testing the dashboard and steering wheel of a 1997 model car, still in the blueprint stage, using an experimental virtual reality system.

You can imagine other uses. Architects could give home buyers the experience of walking through a house still on the drawing board, allowing them to experience the effect of changing a room's size, ceiling height, or style of windows. Students could explore the moon's surface in a lunar vehicle or walk unharmed through a reenacted battle of Gettysburg.

And, as costs go down, virtual reality will settle into the home entertainment market. VCRs and cable TV have proven how enormous that market is.

The last frontier I'll discuss today is the human-machine interface: communicating with computers. Computer command systems have evolved from the punch card to the keyboard to the "mouse" and now special pens used to write instructions on a computer screen. But all this is less natural than simply telling a computer what you want.

Well that day is not far away. At the current rate of progress, we probably will have a talking computer by the year 2001, although it will be a pale imitation of the "Space Odyssey's" HAL.

At AT&T's Bell Laboratories, a computer has been programmed to understand 1,000 words. Our scientists believe in the mid-90s, we will have computers with 5,000-word vocabularies that could take simple dictation. By the turn of the century, computers may have 20,000-word vocabularies, more than the average person, and will be capable of translating foreign languages.

In fact, AT&T and Spain's telephone company demonstrated a rudimentary translation system at the summer Olympics. With a vocabulary of about 450 words relating to money, the system was able to translate requests about the exchange rate of dollars and pesetas in English and Spanish.

Closer to home, a speech recognition system that pulls information from a database is being trialed right now in Arizona. There highway police phone into a computer and speak the driver's license and plate numbers. In seconds, the computer checks a data base and tells them whether the car is stolen or if the driver is wanted.

In the very near future, you will be able to dial your phone by telling it who you want to talk with, and it won't just ring but will tell you who is calling.

Which brings me to the other half of this human-machine equation: computer-synthesized speech. It's a very well developed technology. In fact, you may have talked with such a system already. Speech synthesis and recognition systems are now handling some telephone operator services, such as collect calls, across the country. By the way, if you have any problems talking to the computer, the system will connect you with a human operator at the touch of a button.

For all this progress, it's not clear just when we'll be able to throw away our computer keyboards and converse with a computer as easily as with a person. As complicated as computers are, it turns out human beings are much more complex. But on a pretty basic level we will be conversing with computers and other appliances in ten years or so.

As you've probably noticed, almost all that I've described is off the drawing board and in the laboratory or the marketplace. As Coleridge said: "In today, already walks tomorrow." What I've described is not so much a prediction—what is possible—but rather a technology forecast—what is probable.

And if some of this still seems improbable to you, consider that fifteen or so years ago we didn't have portable phones and fax machines, PCs or CDs, VCRs or microwaves. They've burst on the scene and changed our lives immeasurably.

Arguably, not all of the technological change in that time has been for the better. But, on balance, I'd think most of us would agree technology has improved our lives. Whether the future will be better yet is beyond prediction. It's more a matter of faith.

The progress of communications leads me to cast my lot with the optimists. Over the past 100 years, communication technology had drawn our nation closer together, and helped create a single marketplace, possibly even a single national identity.

Now communication is helping to create a global village, truly democratizing information, making it accessible to everyone, everywhere. The downfall of communism was brought about in good measure because information media penetrated the Iron Curtain, and made the people behind it aware that in other countries people led richer, freer lives.

So while it's wise to regard technology with some suspicion—to accept the Luddite within us—I hope we will keep faith in ourselves because we ultimately control how technology is used.

And I hope you would agree with the philosopher John Dewey who said, "The future is not ominous but a promise; it surrounds the present like a halo."

THE ARTS AND THE AMERICAN DREAM[1]
Barbara Jordan[2]

In what has become a tradition, arts leaders from across the country annually descend on Washington D.C. to discuss the cultural issues facing their communities and the country as a whole. The event, known as Arts Advocacy Day, gives representatives of more than twenty national, state and community arts organizations an opportunity to meet with their congressman. It also allows for the more than 250 members of the bipartisan Congressional Arts Caucus to discuss the cultural priorities of their artistic fields and communities, to examine the range of governmental activity affecting the arts and to set goals for national arts policy.

Arts Advocacy Day 1993, held on March 17, was significant for several reasons. Governmental support of the arts has become a highly controversial issue since a group of senators, in 1989, charged the National Endowment for the Arts with funding photographic exhibits that included, in their opinion, homoerotic and pornographic material. To counter this, the senators introduced legislation to prohibit the NEA from supporting "indecent" or "obscene" works. The controversy culminated in President George Bush asking for the resignation of John E. Frohnmayer, the chairman of the endowment.[3]

Arts Advocacy Day 1993 assumed added importance because of the election of a new President and Congress. Representative Louise M. Slaughter observed:

This session of Congress marks a momentous time for America's cultural community and presents us with a tremendous opportunity. The 103rd Congress, along with a new administration, faces a legislative agenda which promises to have long-lasting implications for our nation's cultural vitality. (*Congressional Record,* March 19, 1993, E715).

[1]Delivered in the Kennedy Center, Washington D.C., on March 16, 1993.
[2]For biographical note, see Appendix.
[3]For speeches related to the controversy, see Kitty Carlisle Hart's "Artistic Freedom and Censorship" and Isabel Allende's "The Power of Art," all in *Representative American Speeches: 1989–1990*, pp. 65–82; John E. Frohnmayer's "Community and the Arts" in *Representative American Speeches: 1990–1991*, pp. 143–150; and Frohnmayer's "Free Expression and Human Rights" in *Representative American Speeches: 1991–1992*, pp. 147–157.

Initiated in 1988, the Nancy Hanks Lecture on Arts and Public Policy, sponsored by the American Council for the Arts, has been an important feature of the annual Arts Advocacy Day. The lecture memorializes Nancy Hanks (1927–1983), who served as chairperson of the National Endowment for the Arts from 1969 to 1977. The 1993 lecturer was Barbara Jordan, former Texas Congresswoman and current Lyndon B. Johnson Centennial Chair in National Policy at the University of Texas at Austin.

Jordan was probably well known to most of her audience. She burst on the national stage in 1974 while serving on the House Judiciary Committee as it was considering articles of impeachment against President Nixon for alleged offenses connected with the Watergate scandal. In 1976, Jordan was chosen to deliver the keynote address to the Democratic National Convention. The keynote speech electrified the hall, and Waldo W. Braden observed that it left little doubt about Jordan's mastery of public speaking. She was one of the few speakers at either national convention to be brought back to the platform by the audience's roar of approval. David Brinkley of NBC commented, "For the first time, the convention has come alive. She is the star." (*Representative American Speeches, 1976–1977*, Waldo W. Braden, editor, pp. 11–12).

Jordan delivered the Nancy Hanks lecture to an audience of arts leaders and supporters from across the country, members of Congress and arts agency leaders in the concert hall of Washington D.C.'s Kennedy Center, on the evening of March 16, 1993.

Barbara Jordan's speech: I am most delighted to be included among the list of distinguished persons who have presented the Nancy Hanks Lecture. Thank you for the honor.

In 1988, Arthur Schlesinger, Jr. gave this lecture. He referred to the well-regarded work he and his father have done in developing and promoting the idea of the cycles of American history. I quote now from his book, which bears that name:

"Wise men have remarked on a pattern of alternation, of ebb and flow, in human history. "The two parties which divide the state, the party of Conservatism and that of Innovation," wrote Emerson in 1841, "are very old, and have disputed the possession of the world ever since it was made . . . Now one, now the other gets the day, and still the fight renews itself as if for the first time, under new names and hot personalities." Innovation presses ever forward; Conservatism holds ever back. We are reformers spring

and summer, in autumn and winter we stand by the old; reformers in the morning, conservers at night. 'Innovation is the salient energy; Conservatism the pause on the last moment.'"
Continuing, from Professor Schlesinger:

Half a century later, Henry Adams applied a more precise version of the cyclical thesis to the first years of the American republic. "A period of about twelve years," he wrote, "measured the beat of the pendulum." After the Declaration of Independence, twelve years had been needed to create an efficient Constitution; another twelve years of energy brought a reaction against the government then created; a third period of twelve years was ending in a sweep toward still greater energy; and already a child could calculate the result of a few more such returns.

We are properly positioned in time, in this year, 1993, to begin a new cycle. Optimism is fairly dropping from the air. A new generation of leaders struggles, at first somewhat awkwardly, to find its sea legs. Old words are coming out of new mouths as we seek to find our niche. This is not a time to be shy. One way to guarantee that this sense of hope will not be lost is to act on it now.

If your thing, that is, your interest, concern, involvement, or passion is the arts, you are probably at this moment in time somewhat reluctant to speak too loudly. With all the rhetoric of budget deficits and sacrifice perhaps you feel that it would be somehow sacrilegious to talk about the arts. Wrong! The arts are an integral part of us and have been often pivotal in reinvigorating our national spirit.

The primary thesis of my remarks today is that the arts, instead of quaking along the periphery of our policy concerns must push boldly into the core of policy. The arts are a response to our individuality and our nature and help to shape our identity. Or as a young student in my class at Laguna Gloria Art Museum in my hometown of Austin, Texas, wrote, "Every feeling comes out on my paper and in my drawings." The arts are not a frill, and should not be treated as such. They have the potential to become the driving force for healing division and divisiveness.

I would guess that few of you in this room think that the arts are a frill. I doubt that you would be here if you held that view. But each of us knows that to further what progress the arts have made as an integral part of American life, we must reason with those who are inclined to consider the arts as one of those things to be dealt with seriously much later on.

I want to offer to you today a premise, with which I hope you agree, that in this time of change in American life, in this new administration of hope, in this time of putting people first, it is the arts that are uniquely placed not just to tag along in the changes, but to be part and parcel of every bold new step we take.

I submit to you the idea that the arts can be the validation of the American life. We heard President Clinton in his address to a joint session of Congress last month speak about renewing our economy so that the American dream can be a possibility for everyone. No one disputes that a healthy economy is part and parcel of the American dream. But it is our job to teach emphatically that the arts are more than just the decorations on that dream.

And what precisely is the American dream? It is: That we are one people.

E Pluribus Unum. The Latin phrase on the great seal of the United States literally translated means one from many. We need to reattach pluribus to unum—the many to the one. That motto challenges our diversity. No nation on the face of the earth had tried so bold an experiment until us, the Americans. No one thought that success would come easily. Even though the founders were aggressive in pursuing liberty, their quest for equality failed to include all. They envisioned no role for former slaves and deferred for a century even thinking about the issue. Even the great democrat of Monticello, Thomas Jefferson, was apprehensive. He, quoting now from a recent *Wall Street Journal* article, "feared that a simple biracial America, white and black as equals, would not long endure. He advocated black freedom, but remained paralyzed by its implications."

Jefferson articulated his quandary regarding slavery when he said, "We have the wolf by the ears and we can neither hold him, nor safely let him go." What frustration!

The arts can help us painlessly to articulate and showcase our oneness. The arts have no pigmentation. The American dream has survived many attacks from our deadliest war to Rodney King. That's a long stretch. To borrow a phrase from William Faulkner, I remain confident it will continue not just to survive, but to prevail over the attacks from extremists of every ilk. Today, we are made uncomfortable by newly awakened conditions of "ethnic cleansing." Why the discomfort? Perhaps we are haunted by our past. Again, we do not know what to do with that wolf.

Assimilation was never the goal of the diverse ethnic groups in America. Inclusion without discomfort is now and ever will be the goal. Maybe one day we will be comfortable enough with each other to drop the hyphens. There should be no hyphenated Americans. The idea of a melting pot was and remains a myth. Universal inclusivity is not a racial idea. The President's Committee on the Arts and the Humanities, writing under the Bush administration, concluded that "American culture incorporates the heritage of many people and thereby provides a unique context for multicultural understanding."

But what is there that can transcend deep differences and stubborn divisions? I suggest: the arts. They have a wonderful universality. Art has the potential to unify. It can speak in many languages without a translator. Art does not discriminate: it ignores external irrelevancies and opts for quality, talent and competence. Let me quote again from the children attending the class at the Austin museum, children who could not have attended without scholarships. When asked if they were surprised at what their classmates had made, as well as what they had made themselves, some of the responses were, "Yes, because I didn't expect to see some of the things I could do," and "Yes, I didn't think I could do it that good," and "I was surprised that all the art work turned out great." Again, art unifies, it does not discriminate.

We are concerned about the economy. We know it has been a deep rut and President Clinton is struggling mightily to find the tools to get us out. We need to make our voices heard with the measure that the arts should not be overlooked in the economic decisions being made today. I applaud our President for seeking to avoid the quick-fix mentality that got us where we are today. It is only in long-term solutions that we will thrive. And I think the arts offer one of these long-term solutions. Yes, this is one of those "radical" ideas spelled out by none other than the last administration's Committee on the Arts and Humanities.

There is no reason, patrons of the arts, to apologize for beauty. But it is important in this time of economic worries to articulate what is obvious to each of us: that art does more than stimulate and please the senses. The arts, in the words of the President's committee, are integrally related to the U.S. economy and contribute to our nation's wealthy, competitiveness, and growth. If we look just at the copyright industries of broadcasting, records and tapes, motion pictures, theatrical productions, newspapers, periodicals, and books, plus computer programming and software, we find a contribution of more than $173 billion, or 3.3 percent of our gross national product. Add art, photography, and architecture and you find a contribution of almost 6 percent to the GNP from the arts, more than food, apparel, chemical, and retailing industries combined.

These figures don't include the economic impact of increased tourism and revitalization of downtown urban areas. Nor do these figures speak to a vital part of the American dream: the arts provide a passage out of poverty for thousands of economically disadvantaged individuals. Professional sports may capture the imaginations of many economically impoverished young people, but the arts—historically more open to all of the diverse segments of our society—provide the careers that can lift young men and women out of poverty.

And why is it that the arts can work this economic magic? It isn't magic, it's common sense. There is a direct relationship between the arts and self-esteem. Again, quoting from the children in the Laguna Gloria museum school: "No one can say your art is ugly because it is in the eyes of the beholder." One child learned "that I could be productive." Self-esteem is a good that each individual cherishes. An artist creates beauty and others enjoy it. He or she gets pleasure in knowing that he is the source of that pleasure and thus, regard for self is enhanced.

Self-esteem is a value which forecloses destructive tendencies; that is, you can not feel good about who you are and where you are and simultaneously destroy your neighborhood. Such a contradiction is inherent and would be personally painful and debilitating.

I have just echoed the thoughts of Jacques Barzun, who in the 1973 Mellon Lectures in Fine Arts, declared that "art is power." He said that art "influences the mind, the nerves, the feelings, the soul" and that it "carries the message of hope, hostility, derision, and moral rebuke. It can fight material and spiritual evils and can transmit the ideals of a community now living, long past, or soon to be born." The arts are a multigenerational communicator.

In order for the arts to live up to the ambitious agenda I have prescribed, those of us who are patrons and supporters must be more than distant observers and appreciative spectators. We need to seek a permanent place in public school curricula for arts education. I commend the *New York Times* for its attention in a number of recent articles entitled "Missing Muses." Those articles point out that art classes teach the very qualities educators can reinvigorate American schools: analytical thinking, teamwork, motivation, and self-discipline.

In Austin, an elementary school teacher is quoted as saying,

"Fine arts is where every child can succeed. It doesn't matter if the child is a genius or a slow learner. You have a natural at-risk program at every school." A school board trustee said, "Public school arts programs are the only outlet that poor people have. While some families can afford private lessons, there are thousands who can't." That trustee was obviously not in the majority when two years ago, the Austin school board cut art and music and physical education classes out of its kindergarten curriculum as one way of balancing its budget. Some of the district's schools have managed to re-institute those classes, but only through extraordinary efforts by teachers, parents and private contributions.

The arts deserve a higher place on America's public policy agenda. Sondra Meyers, the cultural advisor to Pennsylvania's governor, recently wrote:

At this moment of political change—which offers the promise of a people-centered political agenda—we must wake up to the realities of our rich cultural resources and make the case for the integration of culture into public policy. We need to use every asset at our disposal to restore a sense of community and humaneness to our society and culture.

We must, to borrow a phrase from the 1960s, seize the moment that has been handed to us. We are embarking on the first movements in a new cycle in American history. We have just completed a cycle during which the arts survived but only by scratching and clawing to hold the gains of the previous cycle. It is up to those of us in this room to lead the way. We must be sure that our President and the Congress—and the American people most of all—understand that the arts can lift us all up.

I listened on January 20, to Maya Angelou as she captured beauty in language. She said:

Here on the pulse of this new day
You may have the grace to look up and out
And into your sister's eyes and into
Your brother's face, your country
And say simply
Very simply
With hope
Good morning.

I listened; I heard; I believed. Patrons, practitioners, supporters of the arts, I say to you, very simply, with hope, Good morning. Have a very good day.

LEST WE FORGET

THE MEANING OF THE HOLOCAUST TO CHRISTIANS[1]
John C. Danforth[2]

On April 22, 1993, nearly fifty years after the end of World War Two, survivors, relatives, sympathizers and world leaders gathered in Washington D.C. to dedicate the United States Holocaust Memorial Museum. The museum, built with private contributions on federally donated land, stands near the Mall, not far from the Washington Monument.

On the Sunday before the dedication of the museum, Missouri Senator John C. Danforth preached a sermon in commemoration of the holocaust at the Washington National Cathedral. Officially the Cathedral Church of Saints Peter and Paul, it was founded in 1907 by Protestant Episcopalians, and has been the scene of many religious faiths causing it to become known as a truly national church.

The cathedral, funded entirely by private donations, spans a tenth of a mile and is the fifth largest cathedral in the world. Situated atop Mount St. Alban, the District of Columbia's highest point—nearly one hundred feet higher than the Washington Monument, the cathedral overlooks a panoramic view of the city.

It was in this distinguished setting that Senator Danforth delivered his sermon at an ecumenical service on Sunday, April 18, 1993, to an audience of approximately 2500 worshippers of various faiths. A lawyer and an ordained clergyman, Danforth has been described by a Senate colleague as,

. . . one of the most thoughtful and dedicated members of this body. He has served with distinction for many years. His opinions are often sought and highly regarded, and he has played a key role in much of the important legislative business transacted in recent years. (Senator William Cohen, *Congressional Record,* April 28, 1993, s5046).

---

[1]Delivered at the Washington National Cathedral, Washington, D.C., at 11:00 A.M. on Sunday, April 18, 1993.

[2]For biographical note, see Appendix.

John C. Danforth's speech: Fourteen years ago this Cathedral held the first national observance of Days of Remembrance of the Victims of the Holocaust. It was my privilege to preach the sermon.

A year later, President Carter signed a law making Days of Remembrance an annual observance.

This year is especially eventful for two reasons. Tomorrow marks the 50th anniversary of the Warsaw Ghetto Uprising, the symbol of Jewish armed resistance against the Nazis. Secondly, we are dedicating the United States Holocaust Memorial Museum. That structure will guarantee that, for generations to come, Americans will never forget the horrors of the past.

From the beginning, Days of Remembrance have included a Sunday, the Christian day of worship. Christians who helped design Days of Remembrance wanted it that way. They wanted Christians to reflect on the Holocaust and to consider their own responsibility and their own response.

So we meet today, not in an auditorium but in a Christian cathedral, not in an interfaith service, but in the central act of Christian worship. We meet to remember six million Jews—their terrible deaths and the events leading to those deaths. We meet to say what the Holocaust means to us as Christians and what we intend to do as our response.

It is not possible to recognize the magnitude of the Holocaust without admitting the complicity of Christians. Germany, in the 1930s and '40s, was a country of ancient Christian traditions, both Catholic and Protestant. Nothing of any consequence that occurred in that country could have escaped the notice of Christian citizens. Because the Holocaust was so prolonged and so enormous, countless Christians must have participated in it.

Consider the size of the Holocaust. Then ask yourself if Christians were responsible. Nazi persecution of Jews lasted 12 years, from 1933 to 1945. This was no passing phase.

Hitler raved against Jews at mass rallies attended by hundreds of thousands. This was no secret act.

Innumerable people built and guarded death camps, operated gas chambers, and cremated or disposed of bodies. This was a job for multitudes.

Nazis rounded up Jews throughout Europe. Cattle cars filled with Jews crisscrossed the continent. This was a huge and complex task.

In the end, the extermination of Jews became the highest

priority of Nazi Germany. It took precedence over winning the war. This was not the work of a few madmen. It was the mission of a nation, meticulously planned and carefully executed. It defined the purpose of a political system. It engaged the commitment of citizens and soldiers. It could not have been a secret. Those who did it and those who condoned it professed the Christian faith.

How could Christians have done this?

In the summer of 1944, one of the Auschwitz gas chambers was out of order. Therefore, the SS proceeded to kill children by burning them alive on a wood fire. To mask the screams, prison officials ordered an inmate orchestra to play the "Blue Danube."

Of the six million Jews killed in the Holocaust, one million were children. How could Christians have done this?

To answer this, we must see that the Holocaust is not an isolated anomaly. We must see it in context.

This does not mean that the Holocaust is merely another event in the long course of history. It is unique. We should never obscure its horror by comparing it to anything else. It stands alone as the darkest epoch of humankind. Never before or since has absolute evil held such overwhelming sway.

But anti-Semitism did not begin in the 1930s. In the Fourteenth Century, Christians in Europe gave Jews the choice of converting to Christianity or burning alive. In 1648 and '49, programs in Eastern Europe claimed a half million Jewish lives.

And anti-Semitism continues in the 1990s. It continues in our own country. Last year, at Brown University, swastikas and anti-Jewish statements appeared on dormitory doors and in library books.

Last year, at Queens College, New York, dead cats were placed in toilets with graffiti on the wall saying, "We're going to do to Jews what we do to the cats."

This past February, in Fort Lauderdale, Florida, a newspaper ad appeared advertising soap made from Jews.

Thoughtful Christians are asking, what is the cause of this behavior and what can we do about it? Gregory Baum, a Christian student of anti-Semitism wrote, "The Holocaust teaches the Church that any monopolistic claim to divine truth or any form of ecclesiastical self-elevation will eventually translate itself . . . into social attitudes and political action and hence generate grave injustices and eventually accumulate to become major crimes."

This is a good explanation of anti-Semitism, as well as other forms of religious hatred. Any monopolistic claim to divine truth leads to grave injustice and major crimes.

There can be no doubt that this is true. In country after country, it is true today. It is true in Lebanon and in Northern Ireland. It is true in America and Azerbaijan, in Bosnia and Herzegovina. It is true in Sudan and on the West Bank of the Jordan. It is true between Catholics and Protestants, Christians and Muslims, Muslims and Jews.

Killing in the name of God is as old as history. To true believers, it is a cause. To the less religious, it is an excuse. Here is the line of reasoning: I have God's truth. You have rejected God. I have a mission. It is to spread God's truth. You resist me. I will destroy you.

In the Middle Ages, Christians launched crusades in the name of Christ. Claiming Christ's sanction, they took arms against supposed infidels. In this century, supposed Christians, who were followers of Adolf Hitler murdered six million Jews. All this was in the name of or under the cover of the Prince of Peace.

If a monopolistic claim to divine truth leads to holocaust, what are we Christians to do? How are we to respond so as to assure that neither holocaust nor anything like it will ever happen again?

First, we must make it clear that Christians do not have a monopolistic claim to divine truth. We must say, as Cardinal Franz Konig said, "Anti-Semitism has no basis in theology." If Christian theologians have not stated this with sufficient clarity in the past, they must state it forthrightly in the future.

With regard to any monopolistic claim to divine truth, Jesus taught us that we are not to judge others lest we be judged ourselves. We are not to condemn others lest we be condemned ourselves. St. Paul taught us the limitation of our own wisdom. He said that we see through a glass darkly. He said that all people, including the most devout Christians, fall short in the sight of God.

Then there is our responsibility to be ministers of Christ, ambassadors of reconciliation. The Epistle to the Ephesians speaks of Christ who makes peace, who reconciles us to God, who brings hostility to an end. This is the Christ of the New Testament—the Christ who reaches out his arms in love—who embraces humankind. We Christians, clergy and lay, are his ministers, not his warriors or his vigilantes.

Christ has not licensed his followers to abuse other people. The opposite is the case. Listen to the words of Jesus from the Sermon on the Mount:

"You have heard that it was said to the men of old, 'You shall not kill, and whoever kills shall be liable to judgment.' But I say to you that everyone who is angry with his brother shall be liable to judgment. Whoever insults his brother shall be liable to the council, and whoever says, 'You fool!' shall be liable to the hell."

In Christianity, the commandment, "Thou shalt not kill" includes even insults. It includes even calling a person a fool. It certainly includes anti-Semitism in any form. The Christian faith not only does not condone it, the Christian faith forbids it.

The first step, then, is to state clearly that Christians do not monopolize divine truth and that we cannot abuse other people. That is a task for our theologians and our preachers. But what about the ordinary Christian? Surely, the whole answer to the Holocaust is not in the hands of scholars and preachers. The work of holocaust was the work of average men and women. So the work of preventing holocaust should be the work of average men and women. The work of love is more than thinking and speaking. The work is acting.

What can ordinary Christians do to combat holocaust? What actions can we take? Here are three examples. You will be able to think of others.

First, as Christians, we can show an interest in the religious life of Jewish friends. It is a wonderful experience to attend the bar mitzvah of a friend's son, or share a Seder meal at Passover, or, best of all if you can get an invitation, attend an orthodox wedding. If you show an interest, Jews will delight in surrounding you with the warmth of their tradition. Simply knowing people and their beliefs helps prevent meanness and abuse. It is also proof, on a very personal level, that Christians do not monopolize divine truth.

Second, ordinary Christians can actively fight any form of bigotry they encounter. When we hear a hateful word, we can speak out against it. We can let it be known that we do not approve it and do not want to hear it repeated. And, we can do more.

From time to time, we read newspaper accounts of terrible acts to Jews in our own communities. A swastika may be painted on a synagogue or graffiti on a school. It would be a wonderful act of faith and a magnificent statement to the community if Christians arrived within hours, with buckets and scrub brushes, and cleaned up the mess. Christians can do more than say they oppose bigotry. They can show they oppose bigotry.

Third, Christians can seek out specific ways to work with Jews in the service of the broader community. Such a project could be a joint outreach to the inner city or to the homeless. This would not be just another effort by good people to do good works. It would be specifically religious. Jewish and Christian congregations, in concert with each other, would act out their religious commitments to love their neighbors. They would be doing so, in the name of God, not out of a general feeling of good will. If people can kill one another in the name of God, surely they can work together in the name of God. In compassion for the poor and weak, Jews have a lot to teach Christians. The prophetic tradition of social justice is a legacy Jews have given us.

Taking an interest in Jewish religion, active opposition to bigotry, common projects of social outreach—these are three ways in which ordinary Christians can respond to the Holocaust.

The point is not precisely how we respond, but that we respond—in thought, in word and in deed. The point is that we respond to the most dreadful epoch in history, that we respond not because we are good people, but because we are Christians. The point is that we make it our task to assure that neither the Holocaust nor anything like it will ever happen again.

We gather in our cathedral at our regular time of worship. We remember the death of six million Jews. Jewish guests at this service honor us by their presence, for they share with us their special tragedy. Let us make it a point to share more together in years ahead.

At our service in our words Christians respond to the Holocaust. We renounce bigotry in all its forms. We renounce it in the name of Christ.

TRIBUTE TO THURGOOD MARSHALL[1]
Carol Moseley-Braun[2]

On January 26, 1993, the newly-elected United States Senator from Illinois, Carol Moseley-Braun, gave a ten-minute statement to the Senate. Her brief address is significant for three reasons: (1) Moseley-Braun is the first African-American woman elected to the United States Senate; (2) her speech is a eulogy for the recently deceased Thurgood Marshall, the civil rights leader and

[1]Delivered to the United States Senate, Washington, D.C., on January 26, 1993.
[2]For biographical note, see Appendix.

the first black Supreme Court Justice; and (3) it is her maiden Senate speech.

In the hours following Marshall's death on January 24, 1993, admirers and former colleagues found it difficult to name Justice Marshall's most significant contribution to American society because he had made so many. However, the President of Dartmouth College, James Freedman, a former law clerk for Marshall, probably spoke for most people when he identified Marshall's crowning achievement as his successful 1954 litigation of *Brown v. Board of Education,* in which the Supreme Court declared that the doctrine of "separate but equal," the main legal support for racial segregation in public schools, was no longer legal in America.

In her speech to the Senate, Moseley-Braun acknowledged Marshall's contribution to her own life, remarking:

> He certainly made a difference in my life, opening doors of opportunity measured only by merit. He helped ensure that I was able to attend public schools and the University of Chicago Law School, and not schools for blacks only. His work helped my election to the U.S. Senate possible. He opened closed doors and created new opportunities for me and for many, many others. His life was the most convincing evidence that change is possible.

Historically, the first, or "maiden," speech by a new member to the main legislative body—in England, the House of Commons, and in the United States, Congress—was considered crucial to the political career of the speaker. Although such importance is no longer attached to a member's first speech, Braun's remarks drew this response from Illinois Senator Paul Simon:

> I do not know that anyone was aware those were her first comments on the floor of the Senate. I think it is appropriate that Senator Carol Moseley-Braun, who is herself a pioneer, should in her first remarks pay tribute to someone who was a pioneer. (Congressional Record, January 26, 1993, s681).

Carol Moseley-Braun's speech: Mr. President, Thurgood Marshall died last Sunday of heart failure. I still have great difficulty believing it. I know he was born over 84 years ago, and I know that he himself said he was "old and falling apart," but it is nonetheless hard to conceive that a heart as mighty and as courageous as his is no longer beating.

Thurgood Marshall epitomized the best in America; he was, in fact, what this country is all about. That may seem to be an odd thing to say about him. After all, he himself was very aware of the fact that the United States did not, and in too many instances still does not, live up entirely to its founding principles. He knew that the phrases of the Declaration of Independence, "that all men are created equal" and are endowed "with certain inalienable rights," including those to "life, liberty and the pursuit of happiness . . . ," were not, all too much of the time, the principles that govern everyday life in America.

Thurgood Marshall was born in Baltimore in 1908. He lived and felt the humiliation of racism, of not being able even to use the bathroom in downtown Baltimore simply because of the color of his skin.

But Thurgood Marshall was not defeated by racism. He knew that racial inequality was incompatible with American ideals, and he made it his life's unending fight to see that this country's ideals became true for all of its citizens.

And what a fight it has been. It took Thurgood Marshall from Baltimore's segregated public schools to Lincoln University, where he graduated with honors, to Howard University Law School, to the NAACP, to the circuit bench, to the U.S. Solicitor General's office, to become the first African-American member of the U.S. Supreme Court.

That quick biography does not begin to measure the battles Thurgood Marshall fought and won, and the strength, conviction and power he put into the fight.

Thomas Jefferson said that "A little rebellion, now and then, is a good thing, and as necessary in the political world as storms in the physical." Thurgood Marshall took Jefferson at his word, and played a key role in creating a rebellion in America, a rebellion not of violence, but of law. What Marshall did was to use the U.S. legal system to bludgeon and destroy state-supported segregation.

What Marshall did was to use the courts and the law to force the United States to apply the promises made every American in our Declaration of Independence and our Bill of Rights to African-Americans who had little or no protection under the law up until the Marshall legal rebellion. What Marshall did was to make the 13th, 14th, and 15th amendments to our Constitution the law of the land in reality, instead of just an empty promise.

The history of the civil rights movement in this country is, in no small part, the history of Marshall's battles before the Supreme Court. As lead counsel of the National Association for the Advancement of Colored People, Marshall appeared before the Supreme Court 32 times, and won 29 times. His legal skills, grounded in sound preparation and sensitivity to the evidence helped him win such landmark decisions as Smith versus Allwright, Shelley versus Kramer, Sweatt versus Painter, and the biggest case of them all, Brown versus Board of Education.

I am somewhat reluctant to dwell on Thurgood Marshall's many successes, because I know he would not like it. He would not like it because he knew only too well that there are many more battles that must be fought and won if America's founding principles and American reality are to become one and the same for every American of every color. In his dissent in the Bakke case, Marshall said:

The position of the Negro today in America is the tragic but inevitable consequence of centuries of unequal treatment. Measured by any benchmark of comfort or achievement, meaningful equality remains a distant dream for the Negro.

However, the fact that the battle is not yet won does not lessen Marshall's many accomplishments. He was a man who worked and fought to make a difference; he was a man who did make a difference.

He certainly made a difference in my life, opening the doors of opportunity measured only by merit. He helped ensure that I was able to attend public schools and the University of Chicago Law School, and not schools for blacks only. His work helped make my election to the U.S. Senate possible. He opened closed doors and created new opportunities for me and for many, many others. His life was the most convincing evidence that change is possible.

I want to close, Mr. President, by quoting Thurgood Marshall one more time. In the Bakke case, he said:

In light of the sorry history of discrimination and its devastating impact on the lives of Negroes, bringing the Negro into the mainstream of American life should be a state interest of the highest order.

I share his view. Elimination of racism is not just an interest of African-Americans, but of all Americans. Only then will we be able to tap the full potential of our people. Only then will we live the greatness of the American promise.

I hope we will all remember Thurgood Marshall by continuing his lifetime to struggle. I hope we will all remember Marshall by dedicating ourselves to the principles and goals he dedicated himself to: making American opportunity available to every American. And as we work toward those goals, I hope we can all live our lives as completely as he did, enjoy ourselves as much as he did, and poke as much fun at ourselves as Thurgood Marshall did all of his life.

I will miss Thurgood Marshall. America will miss Thurgood Marshall. I am proud to have the opportunity, in some small way, to continue his work, and to try to build on his legacy.

APPENDIX

BIOGRAPHICAL NOTES

ARCHAMBAULT, DAVID LEON (1947–   ). Born, Fort Yates, ND; B.S., Black Hills State College, 1976; M.Ed., Pennsylvania State University, 1983; teacher, assistant principal, principal, Little Wound School, Kylem SD, Pine Ridge Reservation, 1976–84; faculty, United Tribes Technical College, Bismarck, ND, 1984–87; president, Standing Rock College, Ft. Yates, ND, 1987–   ; president, American Indian College Fund, 1991–93; member, board of directors of the American Indian Higher Education Consortium, North Dakota Humanities Council and The North Dakota Indian Arts Association.

BRANCH, TAYLOR (1947–   ). Born, Atlanta, Georgia; B.A., University of North Carolina; Pulitzer prize, history, 1989; National Book Critics Circle award, nonfiction, 1989; editor, *Washington Monthly, Harper's, Esquire;* author, *Parting the Waters: America in the King Years,* 1988.

BUSH, GEORGE HERBERT WALKER (1924–   ). B.A., Yale University, 1948; honorary degrees, Adelphi University, Austin College, Northern Michigan University, Franklin Pierce College, Allegheny College, Beaver College; lieutenant (j.g.), pilot, U.S. Naval Reserve, World War II; decorated, D.F.C., air medals; co-founder, director, Zapata Petroleum Corporation, 1953–59; president, Zapata Off Shore Company, 1959–64, chairman of the board, 1964–66; chairman, Republican Party of Harris County, 1963–64; delegate to Republican National Convention, 1964, 1970; member of the 90th–91st U.S. Congresses, 7th district of Texas; U.S. ambassador to the United Nations, 1971–72; chairman, Republican National Committee, 1973–74; chief, U.S. Liaison Office, Peking, People's Republic of China, 1974–75; director of the Central Intelligence Agency, 1976–77; vice president of the United States, 1981–89; president of the United States, 1989–93; director, 1st International Bank, Ltd., London, 1st International Bank, Houston, Eli Lilley Corporation, Texasgulf, Purolator; chairman, Heart Fund; trustee, Trinity University, Baylor College of Medicine, Phillips Academy. (See also *Current Biography,* 1983.)

CHRISTOPHER, WARREN (1925–   ). Born, Scranton, North Dakota; B.S., University of Southern California, 1945; LL.B., Stanford University, 1949; clerk for Supreme Court Justice William O. Douglas, 1949–1950; senior partner, O'Melveny and Myers, Los Angeles, 1958–67, 1969–76, and 1981–   ; deputy Attorney General, 1967–69; deputy United States Secretary of State, 1977–81; senior advisor to William Clinton presidential campaign, 1992; co-director of transition between Bush and Clinton administrations, 1992–93; United States Secretary of State, 1993– .

CHURCH, FRANK FORRESTER IV (1948–). Born, Boise, Idaho; B.A., with distinction, Stanford University, 1970; M.Div., magna cum laude, Harvard University, 1974, Ph.D., 1978; minister, Unitarian Church of All Souls, New York City, 1978– ; Montgomery Fellow and visiting professor, Dartmouth College, 1989; author and editor of more than twenty books, including *Father and Son: A Personal Biography of Senator Frank Church of Idaho by His Son*, 1985, *The Devil and Dr. Church*, 1986, *Entertaining Angels*, 1987, *The Essential Tillich*, 1987, *The Seven Deadly Virtues*, 1989, *God and Other Famous Liberals: Reclaiming the Politics of America*, 1992; articles on New Testament studies, the history of early Christianity, the history of liberal religion, and contemporary theological topics.

CLINTON, BILL (WILLIAM JEFFERSON) (1946–). Born, Hope, Arkansas; B.S., Georgetown University, 1968; Rhodes Scholar, Oxford University, 1968–70; J.D., Yale University, 1973; professor, University of Arkansas Law School, 1973–76; Attorney General of Arkansas, 1977–79; Governor of Arkansas, 1979–81, 1983–92; counsel, Wright, Lindsey, & Jennings, Little Rock, 1981–82; president of the United States, 1993– ; chairman, Education Commission of the States, 1986–87; chairman, Democratic Leadership Council, 1990–91.

DANFORTH, JOHN DAGGETT (1936–). Born St. Louis; B.A. Princeton, 1958; B.D. Yale University, 1963, LL.B. 1963; with firm of Davis, Polk, Wardwell, Sunderland, and Kiendi, New York, 1964–66, Bryan, Cave, McPhintees, and McRoberts, St. Louis, 1966–68; Attorney General of Missouri, 1969–1976; US Senator from Missouri, 1976– ; recipient of Distinguished Service award, St. Louis Junior Chamber of Commerce, 1976; World Without Hunger award, 1985, Young Man of Missouri Junior Chamber of Commerce award, 1968; alumni fellow, Yale University, 1973–79.

EITZEN, DAVID STANLEY (1934–). Born, Glendale, California; B.A., Bethel College, 1956; M.S., Emporia State University, 1962; M.A., University of Kansas, 1966, Ph.D., 1968; recreational therapist, Menninger Foundation, 1956–58; teacher, Galva High School (Kansas), 1958–60, Turner High School (Kansas), 1960–65; assistant professor, University of Kansas, 1968–72, associate professor, 1972–74; professor, Colorado State University, 1974– ; president, North American Society for the Sociology of Sport, 1986–87; executive council, Western Social Science Association, 1978–84; chair, Theory Division, Society for the Study of Social Problems, 1986–88; executive council, section on Undergraduate Education, American Sociological Association, 1987–90; member, International Sociological Association, American Sociological Association, Midwest Sociological Society, Society for the Study of Social Problems, Western Social Science Association, International Committee for the Sociology of Sport, North American Society for the Sociology of Sport, American Society of Criminology; Distinguished Alumnus award, Emporia State University, 1989; special recognition for contributions to the Western Social Science

Association on its 30th Anniversary, 1988; Excellence in Research and Creativity, College of Arts, Humanities and Social Sciences, Colorado State University, 1988; N.D.E.A. Fellow, 1965–67; Editor, *The Social Science Journal*, 1978–84; author, *Social Structure and Social Problems in America*, 1974, *Sociology of North American Sport* (with George H. Sage), 1978, *In Conflict and Order*, 1978, *Sport in Contemporary America* (ed.), 1979, *Social Problems*, 1980, *Elite Deviance* (with David R. Simon), 1982, *Criminology* (with Doug A. Timmer), 1985, *Diversity in American Families* (with Maxine Baca Zinn), 1987, *Crime in the Streets and Crime in the Suites* (ed., with Doug A. Timmer), 1989, *The Reshaping of America* (ed., with Maxine Baca Zinn), 1989, and *Society's Problems* (ed.), 1989; over 100 articles in professional journals and chapters in scholarly books.

GERETY, TOM (1946–   ). Born, New York, New York; B.A., Yale University, 1969, M.Phil., 1974, J.D., 1976, Ph.D., 1976; assistant professor, Chicago Kent College Law, Illinois Institute of Technology, 1976–78; professor, law, University of Pittsburgh, 1978–86; Nippert professor, dean of law, University of Cincinnati, 1986–89; president, professor, Trinity College, 1989–   .

JORDAN, BARBARA CHARLINE (1936–   ). Born, Houston, Texas; B.A., Texas Southern University, 1956; LL.B., Boston University, 1959; honorary doctorate degrees from 29 schools including Harvard University, Princeton University, Notre Dame University, Brandeis University, William and Mary, Wake Forest University, and Tuskegee Institute; private legal practice, Houston, 1960–66; member, Texas State Legislature, 1966–72; member, United States House of Representatives, 1972–78; public service professor, Lyndon B. Johnson School of Public Affairs, Austin, Texas, 1979–82; Centennial Chair in National Policy, 1982–   ; keynote address, Democratic National Convention, 1976; Host, "Crisis to Crisis with Barbara Jordan," PBS television series, 1982; Charles Evans Hughes gold metal, National Conference of Christians and Jews, 1987; Harry S. Truman Public Service award, 1990; Elmer B. Staats Public Service Careers award, 1990; Tom C. Clark Equal Justice Under Law award, 1991; Bess Wallace Truman award, 1992; Eleanor Roosevelt Val-Kill medal, 1992; N.A.A.C.P. Springarn award, 1992; Nelson Mandela Award for Health and Human Rights, 1993; *The Great Society: A Twenty-Year Critique* (ed. with Elspeth Rostow), 1986.

MOSELEY-BRAUN, CAROL E. (1947–   ). Born, Chicago, Illinois; B.A., University of Illinois, Chicago, 1969; J.D., University of Chicago, 1972; law clerk, 1970–71; associate, Davis, Miner, and Barnhill, 1972; assistant attorney, United States Department of Justice of Illinois, 1973–1977; Illinois state representative, 1977–1992; Cook County recorder of deeds/registrar of titles; United States Senate, 1993–   ; recipient of several public service, legislative official, and education awards.

NOLAN, JOSEPH THOMAS (1920–   ). Born, Waterbury, Connecticut; A.B., Holy Cross College, 1942; M.A., Boston University, 1945; Ph.D., New York University, 1973; Washington correspondent, United States Press International, 1943–49; writer, copy editor, *The New York Times*, 1949–55;

manager, editorial and press services, R.C.A. Corporation, 1955–62; senior vice president corporate communications, Chase Manhattan Bank, 1962–74; professor, journalism and public affairs, University of South Carolina, 1974–76; vice president public affairs, Monsanto Corporation, 1976–85; Gannett visiting professor of communications, University of Florida, 1985–86; Professor of Communications, University of North Florida, 1986– ; member, Public Relations Society of America.

RAWLINGS, HUNTER RIPLEY, III (1944–). Born, Norfolk, Virginia; B.A., Haverford College, 1966; Ph.D., Princeton University, 1970; assistant professor, University of Colorado, 1970–74, associate professor, 1975–80, professor, 1980–88, vice president academic affairs, Dean System Graduate School, 1984–88: president, University of Iowa, 1988– ; chair, Iowa Commission on Foreign Language Studies and International Education, 1988–91; junior fellow, Center for Hellenic Studies, 1975–76; member, American Philosophy Association, Classical Association, Archeology Association, Ancient Historians, American Association of Universities; editor-in-chief, *Classical Journal,* 1977– ; author, *The Structure of Thucydides History,* 1981.

SAGAN, CARL EDWARD (1934–). Born, New York City; B.A., University of Chicago, 1954, B.S., 1955, M.S., 1956, Ph.D., 1960; D.Sc. (honorary), Rensselaer Polytechnic Institute, 1975, Denison University, 1976, Clarkson College, 1977; D.H.L. (honorary), Skidmore College, 1976; research fellow, University of California, Berkeley, 1960–62; visiting assistant professor, Stanford Medical School, 1962–63; Smithsonian Astrophysics Observatory, 1962–68; lecturer and then assistant professor, Harvard University, 1962–68; member of faculty, Cornell University, 1967– , professor 1970– , David Duncan professor of physical sciences, 1976– , director of Laboratory of Planetary Studies, 1968– , visiting professor and guest lecturer, various colleges and universities; lecturer for the Apollo flight crews of NASA, 1969–72; narrator, BBC/PBL television production, "The Violent Universe," 1969; recipient, Smith Prize, Harvard, 1964, NASA medal for scientific achievement, 1972, Prix Galabert, 1973, John Campbell Award, 1974, Klumpke-Roberts Prize, 1974, Priestley Award, 1975, NASA Award for Public Service, 1977, Pulitzer Prize for *The Dragons of Eden,* 1978; National Science fellow, 1955–60, Sloan Research fellow, 1963–67; author *Atmospheres of Mars and Venus,* 1961, *Planets,* 1966, *Intelligent Life in the Universe,* 1966, *Planetary Exploration,* 1970, *Mars and the Mind of Man,* 1973, *The Cosmic Connecticut,* 1973, *Other Worlds,* 1975, *The Dragons of Eden,* 1977, *Murmurs of Earth: The Voyager Interstellar Record,* 1978, *Broca's Brain,* 1979, *Cosmos,* 1980, *Contact,* 1985, *Comet,* 1985; editor and author of various articles in scientific and astronomy journals. (See also *Current Biography,* 1970.)

TOBIAS, RANDALL L. (1941–). Born, Lafayette, Indiana; B.S., Indiana University, 1964; L.L.D., Gallaudet University; US Army, 1st Lieutenant, 1964–66; vice president residence marketing sales and service, AT&T, 1981–82; president, American Bell Consumer Products, 1983: president, Consumer Products, 1983–84; senior vice president, AT&T Communications, 1984–85; chairman, chief executive officer, AT&T Communications, 1985–91; chairman, chief executive officer, AT&T International, 1991–   ; chairman, national campaign, Indiana University Annual Fund Drive, 1984–85; trustee, Duke University, Colonial Williamsburg Foundation; member, Bretton Woods Commission, Council on Foreign Relations, Well House Society, National Action Council for Minorities in Engineering, Blue Key, Theta Chi.

CUMULATIVE SPEAKER INDEX

1990–1993

A cumulative author index to the volumes of *Representative American Speeches* for the years 1937–1938 through 1959–1960 appears in the 1959–1960 volume, for the years 1960–1961 through 1969–1970 in the 1969–1970 volume, for the years 1970–1971 through 1979–1980 in the 1979–1980 volume, and for the years 1980–1981 through 1989–1990 in the 1989–1990 volume.

INDEX TO VOLUME 65 (1993)
BY SUBJECT

The Breakup of Communism (65:1)
The United Nations' Role in World Affairs (65:2)
Banking Scandals: The S & Ls and BCCI (65:3)
Drugs in America (65:4)
Women's Issues (65:5)
Representative American Speeches (65:6)

AMERICA

The arts and the American dream. B. Jordan. Speech delivered
Mr. 16, '93. **65:6**

Discovery and exploration
Moral and religious aspects

Columbus plus 500 years. D. Archambault. *Vital Speeches of the Day*
Je. 1, '92. **65:6**

AMERICAN CONTINENTAL CORP.
About

Good timing, Charlie. H. Rudnitsky. *Forbes* N. 27, '89. **65:3**

ANTI-SEMITISM

Columbus plus 500 years. D. Archambault. *Vital Speeches of the Day*
Je. 1, '92. **65:6**

U.N. repeals Zionism-is-racism resolution. L. S. Eagleburger. *U.S. Department of State Dispatch* D. 23, '91. **65:2**

BANK OF CREDIT AND COMMERCE INTERNATIONAL
About

A bank of scandal. M. McDonald. *Maclean's* Ag. 5, '91. **65:3**

BCCI and Iran/contra. C. Byron. *New York* N. 25, '91. **65:3**

The big muddy. C. Byron. *New York* Je. 24, '91. **65:3**

Caught in the money-laundry wringer. *U.S. News & World Report*
O. 24, '88. **65:3**

The CIA and BCCI. T. Morganthau. *Newsweek* Ag. 12, '91. **65:3**

Feeling the heat. J. Greenwald. *Time* Ag. 5, '91. **65:3**

Gambling big to nail Noriega. G. DeGeorge. *Business Week* F. 19, '90. **65:3**

Lessons from BCCI. R.E. Norton. *Fortune* S. 9, '91. **65:3**

Morgenthau's mission. J. Schwartz and R. Thomas. *Newsweek* Ag. 10, '92.
65:3

CHILD DAY CARE

Costs

What price child care? J.E. Ellis, et al. *Business Week* F. 8, '93. **65:5**

CHILD WELFARE

National security. D.S. Eitzen. *Vital Speeches of the Day* Mr. 1, '93. **65:6**

CHILDREN OF DRUG ADDICTS

Innocent victims A. Toufexis. *Time* My. 13, '91. **65:4**

Should we take away their kids? J. Willwerth. *Time* My. 13, '91. **65:4**

U.S. foreign relations. W. Christopher. *Vital Speeches of the Day*
Ap. 15, '93. **65:6**

CIVIL RIGHTS

The drug war on civil liberties. D. Baum. *Nation* Je. 29, '92. **65:4**

Colombia

Colombia's dirty war, Washington's dirty hands. R. Conniff. *Progressive*
My. '92. **65:4**

Cuba

Double standard for human rights. M.T. Valdés. *Progressive* Ag. '92. **65:2**

Guatemala

Double standard for human rights. M.T. Valdés. *Progressive* Ag. '92. **65:2**

CIVIL RIGHTS ACT OF 1991

About

Cultural fascism. J.S. McCarthy. *Forbes* D. 9, '91. **65:2**

CIVIL RIGHTS MOVEMENT

Democracy in an age of denial. T. Branch. Speech delivered My. 7, '92.
65:6

Shall we overcome? F.F. Church. Speech delivered Ja. 17, '93. **65:6**

CIVIL SERVICE

International aspects

The fluctuating fortunes of the United Nations international civil service.
R.S. Jordan. *Public Administration Review* Jl./Ag. '91. **65:2**

Rethinking international governance. H. Cleveland. *Futurist* My./Je. '91.
65:2

CLINTON, BILL

American renewal (Inaugural address). B. Clinton. *Vital Speeches of the Day*
F. 15, '93. **65:6**

State of the Union 1993. B. Clinton. *Vital Speeches of the Day* Mr. 15, '93.
65:6

Public relations

The presidency and public opinion. J. Nolan. *Vital Speeches of the Day* Ja.
15, '93. **65:6**

Colombia

Colombia's dirty war, Washington's dirty hands. R. Conniff. *Progressive* My. '92. **65:4**

Latin America

Caught in the money-laundry wringer. *U.S. News & World Report* O. 24, '88. **65:3**

The newest war. C. Lane. *Newsweek* Ja. 6, '92. **65:4**

U.S. drug policy: a bad export. E.A. Nadelmann. *Foreign Policy* Spring '88. **65:4**

Panama

Gambling big to nail Noriega. G. DeGeorge. *Business Week* F. 19, '90. **65:3**

Noriega in Miami. M. Massing. *Nation* D. 2, '91. **65:4**

Peru

Sowing violence in Peru. R. Kirk. *Progressive* Jl. '91. **65:4**

NARCOTICS TRADE

Coke Inc.: inside the big business of drugs. M. Stone. *New York* Jl. 16, '90. **65:4**

History

The men who created crack. G. Witkin. *U.S. News & World Report* Ag. 19, '91. **65:4**

Bolivia

Bolivia: the politics of cocaine. M. Burke. *Current History* F. '91. **65:4**

Colombia

New kings of coke. E. Shannon. *Time* Jl. 1, '91. **65:4**

NATIONALISM

The perils of the new nationalism. E.J. Hobsbawm. *Nation* N. 4, '91. **65:1**

Splinter, splinter little state. G.J. Church. *Time* Jl. 6, '92. **65:1**

NEW WORLD ORDER

The U.N. in a new world order. B.M. Russett and J.S. Sutterlin. *Foreign Affairs* Spring '91. **65:1**

What new world order? J.S. Nye, Jr. *Foreign Affairs* Spring '92. **65:1**

NEW YORK (N.Y.)

Crime

Coke Inc.: inside the big business of drugs. M. Stone. *New York* Jl. 16, '90. **65:4**

Criminal justice, Administration of

Morgenthau's mission. J. Schwartz and R. Thomas. *Newsweek* Ag. 10, '92. **65:3**

NINETEEN HUNDRED AND NINETY-TWO

Power and the glory. *Newsweek* D. 28, '92. **65:5**

Officials and employees

The fluctuating fortunes of the United Nations international civil service. R.S. Jordan. *Public Adminstration Review* Jl./Ag. '91. **65:2**

Israel

U.N. repeals Zionism-is-racism resolution. L.S. Eagleburger. *U.S. Department of State Dispatch* D. 23, '91. **65:2**

Japan

Japan, the United Nations, and human rights. J.M. Peek. *Asian Survey* Mr. '92. **65:2**

Persian Gulf region

The U.N. in a new world order. B.M. Russett and J.S. Sutterlin. *Foreign Affairs* Spring '91. **65:2**

United States

Why the right loves the U.N. I. Williams. *Nation* Ap. 13, '92. **65:2**

UNITED NATIONS. COMMISSION ON HUMAN RIGHTS

About

Double standard for human rights. M.T. Valdés. *Progressive* Ag. '92. **65:2**

UNITED NATIONS. SECURITY COUNCIL (MEETINGS: 1992)

About

Can the U.N. stretch to fit its future? T. Daley. *Bulletin of the Atomic Scientists*. Ap. '92. **65:2**

UNITED NATIONS AND THE PRESS

The U.N.: impact grows, coverage lags. M.J. Berlin. *Washington Journalism Review* O. '92. **65:2**

UNITED NATIONS DEVELOPMENT PROGRAM

About

Why the right loves the U.N. I. Williams. *Nation* Ap. 13, '92. **65:2**

UNITED STATES

Armed Forces

Forces in Latin America

The newest war. C. Lane. *Newsweek* Ja. 6, '92. **65:4**

Economic policy

State of the Union 1993. B. Clinton. *Vital Speeches of the Day* Mr. 15, '93. **65:6**

Foreign relations

America's role in the world. G.H.W. Bush. *U.S. Department of State Dispatch* Ja. 11, '93. **65:6**

U.S. foreign relations. W. Christopher. *Vital Speeches of the Day* Ap. 15, '93. **65:6**

What new world order? J.S. Nye, Jr. *Foreign Affairs* Spring '92. **65:6**

Central Asia
Dateline Tashkent: post-Soviet Central Asia. J. Rupert. *Foreign Policy* Summer '92. **65:6**
Eastern Europe
From Sarajevo to Sarajevo. C. Gati. *Foreign Affairs* Fall '92. **65:1**
Social policy
National security. D.S. Eitzen. *Vital Speeches of the Day* Mr. 1, '93. **65:6**
Urban policy
National security. D.S. Eitzen. *Vital Speeches of the Day* Mr. 1, '93. **65:6**
UNITED STATES. CENTRAL INTELLIGENCE AGENCY
About
The CIA and BCCI. T. Morganthau. *Newsweek* Ag. 12, '91. **65:3**
UNITED STATES. CONGRESS. SENATE. COMMITTEE ON THE JUDICIARY
About
Judging Thomas. G. Borger. *U.S. News & World Report* O. 21, '91. **65:5**
UNITED STATES CONGRESS. SENATE. SELECT COMMITTEE ON ETHICS
About
House of ill-repute. *Nation.* D. 31, '90. **65:3**
Nominees
Judging Thomas. G. Borger. *U.S. News & World Report* O. 21, '91. **65:5**

URBAN ISSUES
Saving our cities. T. Gerety. Speech delivered My. 17, '92. **65:6**
WAGE DIFFERENTIALS
The wage war against women. M. Morris. *Working Mother* Je. '92. **65:5**
When will women get to the top? A.B. Fisher. *Fortune* S. 21, '92. **65:5**
WOMEN
Employment
The myth of the miserable working woman. R.C. Barnett and C. Rivers. *Working Woman* F. '92. **65:5**
The wage war against women. M. Morris. *Working Mother* Je. '92. **65:5**
When will women get to the top? A.B. Fisher. *Fortune* S. 21, '92. **65:5**
Who helps working women care for the young and the old? B. Sancier and P. Mapp. *Affilia.* Summer '92. **65:5**
Working women's staunchest allies: supply and demand. G.S. Becker. *Business Week* D. 2, '91. **65:5**
Legal status, laws, etc.
Should we take away their kids? J. Willwerth. *Time* My. 13, '91. **65:4**

Political activities

Did America 'get it'?. E. Salholz. *Newsweek* D. 28 '92. **65:5**

Power and the glory. *Newsweek* D. 28, '92. **65:5**

WOMEN CONSTRUCTION WORKERS

Creating change by committee. J.M. Stasch. *Working Woman* Ap. '92. **65:5**

WOMEN IN MASS MEDIA

The myth of the miserable working woman. R.C. Barnett and C. Rivers. *Working Woman* F. '92. **65:5**

WOMEN POLITICAL CANDIDATES

Crashing the locker room. W. Kaminer. *Atlantic* Jl. '92. **65:5**

The year of the women. W. McGurn. *National Review* Jl. 6, '92. **65:5**

WOMEN PUBLIC OFFICERS

Power and the glory. *Newsweek* D. 28, '92. **65:5**

WORLD POLITICS

The cold war and its aftermath. Z. Brezezinski. *Foreign Affairs* Fall '92. **65:1**

Whose collective security? E.C. Luck and T. Traister Gati. *The Washington Quarterly* Spring '92. **65:2**

YELTSIN, BORIS

About

Why not try democracy? T. Vorozheikina. *Nation* My. 4, '92. **65:1**

YUGOSLAVIA

Civil War, 1991–

From Sarajevo to Sarajevo. C. Gati. *Foreign Affairs* Fall '92. **65:1**

ZIONISM

U.N. repeals Zionism-is-racism resolution. L.S. Eagleburger. *U.S. Department of State Dispatch* D. 23, '91. **65:2**